DEAR CITIZEN MATH

HOW MATH CLASS CAN INSPIRE A MORE RATIONAL AND RESPECTFUL SOCIETY

KARIM ANI

ISBN (hardback): 978-1-7364085-3-7
ISBN (paperback): 978-1-7364085-1-3
ISBN (ebook): 978-1-7364085-2-0

First printed in the United States in 2021

Editor: Katherine Bryant
Interior Design: Alison Fort
Cover Illustration: Nigel Buchanan
Cover Layout: Mayfly Design

Damascus Rodeo
www.damascusrodeo.com

CONTENTS

PART ONE

MATH CLASS IN THE AGE OF CERTAINTY

Dear Citizen Math,

N August of 2009 I attended a town hall meeting about the Affordable Care Act in Reston, Virginia. At the time, Congress was debating legislation which promised to transform American health care. Across the country, citizens gathered in school gyms, libraries, and city halls to discuss the proposed changes, and tensions that summer were running high.

One of the most popular aspects of the legislation was the requirement that insurance companies could no longer deny health care coverage to people with pre-existing conditions. One of the most controversial aspects was the individual mandate, the requirement that everyone in the country buy insurance or pay a fine. While some viewed this as a necessary tradeoff for requiring companies to cover everyone, others saw it as an example of government overreach. The purpose of the town halls that summer was to give communities an opportunity to hear from their elected representatives and to discuss their concerns with one another thoughtfully and respectfully.

At least that's what was supposed to happen. In Tampa, opponents of the bill shut the discussion down by banging on doors and chanting "tyranny!" On Long Island, police had to escort a congressman to his car when protests turned violent. Protestors in Texas waved signs depicting President Obama with a Hitler mustache, while those in Maryland hanged a congressman in effigy.

As captured by evening news broadcasts showing sidewalk fistfights and newspaper headlines describing "Health Debate Turns Hostile," America that summer looked like a citizenry at war with itself.

As I entered the gymnasium of Reston's South Lakes High School, I was confident that our meeting would be different. Just west of the nation's capital, the Northern Virginia suburb is one of the country's most well-educated regions, a distinction which I assumed would bode well for a constructive health care debate. On top of that was my own state pride. "We're Virginians," I thought as I found a chair near half court. "We wrote the Declaration of Independence and are the literal headquarters of Central Intelligence. Surely our discussion will be thoughtful." Flanked by American flags on a stage in the front of the gym, a local rabbi rose to offer an opening prayer. "We seek among our citizens tonight a true engagement in this debate," he said to the more than 2,000 of us in attendance. "And to approach one another this evening with respect [and] civility." As a former middle school math teacher, I found this a reasonable request. Civility and respect are exactly what I'd expected of my students, and I was sure that my neighbors and I would honor the rabbi's request.

Yet before he even said "Amen," the booing had already begun. People jumped to their feet to jut angry fingers in their neighbors' chests. A man behind me glared red-faced at someone a few rows away, spittle flicking from his lips as he accused them of being a communist. We had gathered to discuss health insurance. But what resulted wasn't a debate, it was a cage fight: a counterproductive venting of ill-informed anger. In 1776, the Founding Fathers gathered in Philadelphia to declare independence from a king and launch our experiment in self-governance. On a basketball court in Virginia more than two centuries later, all I could wonder was, "How much longer will this experiment last?"

Mathematics and the Language of Logic

If you're reading this, there's a good chance that you're involved in American math education. Perhaps you're a classroom teacher. Perhaps you're a curriculum coordinator or an instructional specialist. Or maybe you're a school principal, a district superintendent, or a professor in a college of education. Whatever role you play, if you have influence over the direction of American math instruction, then the future of our democracy may rest in your hands.

As a country, we have a hard time addressing the challenges we face. Instead of debating issues like health insurance rationally, we often approach them dogmatically, emotionally, and unmoored from evidence. More than a decade ago, the problem with our health care debate wasn't that we disagreed with one another's arguments or found opposing perspectives unreasonable. It was that we weren't even making arguments and had abandoned reason altogether. In the years since, our challenges — and our discourse — have only gotten worse. As I write this letter, we are suffering the worst pandemic in more than a century; every day thousands of Americans are dying from COVID-19. Meanwhile, millions are suffering the apocalyptic consequences of rising global temperatures, stronger hurricanes, and out-of-control wildfires. And yet rather than seek to understand such issues so that we might solve them, we scream at one another about whether the coronavirus is a scam and whether climate change denial is a corporate conspiracy. If we as a nation are to address the problems that we share, then we must get better at thinking about them rationally. Mathematics can help us do that, and the math classroom is where we should start.

I realize that strengthening self-governance is not something that most people associate with math education. I was a teacher, too. I taught eighth-grade algebra in rural Virginia and New York City, was a middle school math coach, have a master's degree in secondary math education, and have attended hundreds of department meetings and professional development workshops. Throughout my career in mainstream math education, I learned a lot about how to make connections between tables, graphs, and equations. I was taught how to write classroom learning objectives. I was never told, however, that one of those objectives included saving American democracy. As far as I knew, incubating a thoughtful citizenry was not part of my job description.

I wish it had been. And if you're a math educator now, I hope you'll embrace it as part of yours. For if there's anyone in the country with the power to kindle a commitment to reason, it's you. Consider the questions we face. *Should every American be required to buy health insurance? Should the federal government increase the minimum wage? Do we see evidence of climate change? Is excessive use of force by police a widespread problem or a case of a few bad apples?* Each of these issues is inherently mathematical, which is to say, better understood through the prism of math. A rigorous debate about any of these topics would be incomplete without math.

Take health insurance. Unpaid medical bills are the leading cause of personal bankruptcy in the United States, and tens of thousands of people die each year due to inadequate access to health care. As an issue, health insurance is both critical and fundamentally mathematical. The decision to purchase health insurance comes down to probabilities. If someone has a high probability of getting sick or injured in a given year, insurance will be worth a lot. If someone has a lower probability, insurance will be worth less. If an insurance pool is mostly populated with high-risk customers, the price of insurance will be high. The more low-risk customers the pool can attract, the cheaper insurance will become.

As Congress debated the Affordable Care Act, surveys found that a majority of Americans agreed that insurance companies should not be allowed to deny coverage based on pre-existing conditions. According to experts, there were two main options for how to accomplish this within a system of private insurance. One was to continue to allow individuals to decide for themselves whether or not to buy insurance. In this case, low-risk customers could opt out of the insurance pool if they didn't think a policy was worth the price. If they got sick or injured, hospitals would still provide emergency care. They'd simply raise their prices and pass the costs on to insurance companies. Insurance companies in turn would likely respond by charging more for a policy...prompting many moderate-risk customers to opt out of the insurance pool...prompting insurance companies to raise the price even further. This cycle of increasing prices and declining enrollment is what economists call the "death spiral." In theory, the best way to prevent the insurance pool from boiling over is to require low-risk customers to join it. This was our second option, and the one codified in the Affordable Care Act. By mandating that every individual in America buy a health care plan, the government could ensure that the price remained stable and the market remained sustainable. Of course, the mandate also guaranteed that millions of people would be forced to pay for something that they didn't want.

So what to do? Insurance markets depend on having a large pool of customers with diverse risk profiles. At the same time, the United States is a country founded on the promise of individual liberty. So what's the best way to create a functional insurance system while still honoring personal autonomy?

It's a difficult question. And to be honest, I'm not sure where I come down. But I am sure of two things: first, that any productive discussion about health care must involve probabilities; and second, that the discussion that we were having as a country in 2009 — and the one we continue to have today — did not. We yelled a lot about socialism and "killing grandma," but we reasoned much less about math. Even if we had allowed the logic of mathematical analysis to inform our insurance debates, we wouldn't have necessarily agreed about the right outcome. But at least we would have disagreed constructively. At least we would have been clear on what we were disagreeing about.

Mathematics is a tool that allows us to think more clearly about the questions that we confront as a society. *Should every American be required to buy insurance?* Debating this requires expected value. *Should the government increase the minimum wage?* Discussing this demands systems of linear equations. *Do we see evidence that global temperatures have risen over the past century?* Answering this involves sinusoidal functions. *Is excessive use of force by police a widespread problem or is it limited to a handful of officers?* Though repairing the trust between police departments and the communities they serve is a complex challenge, whatever the solution is, it begins with distributions of data. As a citizenry, we face a wide range of challenges. If we're to successfully address them, we need to get better at analyzing them. Math can help us do that.

Media and the Calcification of Certainty

More than two centuries ago, a collection of colonists in Philadelphia launched an experiment in self-governance, and that's exactly what America is: a test to determine whether We the People can successfully manage ourselves. If our endeavor is to succeed, then we must be willing to approach the challenges we share rationally and ground our disagreements in a common understanding of reality. Unfortunately, as we've witnessed in recent years, our national discourse has become characterized less by reason and civility than by hyper-partisan hyperventilating. In fact, one of the few things we do seem to agree on these days is how much we disagree. Today, 85% of American adults think our discourse has become more negative in recent years, and 75% say it's become less grounded in fact.

In a letter to a friend, Thomas Jefferson once wrote, "Were it left to me to decide whether we should have a government without newspapers, or newspapers without a government, I should not hesitate a moment to prefer the latter." A well-functioning democracy depends on a well-informed citizenry, and well-informed citizens depend on information sources that expose them to new and different ideas. This is the role that journalism and the media are supposed to play in a vibrant democracy: expanding our understanding of the world and supporting us in thinking critically about it.

In recent years, however, some cable news broadcasters and social media platforms that many of us turn to for information have largely done the opposite. Instead of broadening our perspectives on issues like health care and climate change, they narrow them by reaffirming what we already believe. The more the news media have come to reinforce viewers' ideologies, the more

Americans have come to occupy completely separate realities. When it comes to climate change, for instance, a 2019 analysis of the right-leaning Fox News found that 86% of segments that discussed the issue were dismissive or cast doubt on its long-term impacts. The left-leaning MSNBC, on the other hand, tends to present climate change as an immediate and incontrovertible crisis. Perhaps it's no surprise, then, that more than twice as many Republicans as Democrats think that policies aimed at reducing the effects of climate change do more harm than good. In the early days of COVID-19, conservative and progressive broadcasters often covered the outbreak in opposite ways...and their viewers came to opposite conclusions. Two-thirds of MSNBC viewers thought the virus came about naturally (as opposed to having been engineered in a lab), while fewer than one-third of Fox News viewers did. 29% of Fox News viewers believed that a vaccine would be available within a year of the outbreak, compared to only 9% of MSNBC viewers. Driven largely by ideological presentations of the news, Americans don't just disagree about how the world *should* work. More and more, we disagree about how it *does* work.

Our journalistic landscape wasn't always so polarized. Half a century ago, most Americans got their news from three main sources: ABC, NBC, and CBS. These broadcasters viewed a non-partisan newscast as a public service, and anchors such as Walter Cronkite were among the most trusted figures in the country. The networks weren't perfect; in the early years of the Vietnam War, for instance, they succumbed to government pressure to present the conflict more favorably than it warranted, and their race and gender homogeneity did not reflect the diversity of the national population. Still, when it came to presenting current events, the so-called Big Three prioritized objective reality over viewer preferences, an approach made possible by the fact that news broadcasts were not expected to earn a profit.

This changed with the rise of advertising-driven cable news. In 2019 alone, Fox News and MSNBC combined for nearly $2 billion worth of ad sales, thanks in part to their emotion-stoking presentation of the news. Yet as profitable as this strategy is, it's dangerous. It creates a situation where Americans at different ends of the ideological spectrum don't just view one another as being wrong. They accuse one another of being bad: traitorous, treasonous, even evil. Perhaps it's no surprise, then, that Americans are more divided now than at any time in the past quarter century. Unlike in previous eras in which personal affections transcended party affiliations, a quarter of Republicans today say they'd never date a liberal, while nearly half of Democrats say the same about conservatives. In Latin, the word "patria" refers to the nation that we share, and yet more and more of us are coming to define "patriotism" as hating half the people in it.

The internet is even worse. If a television viewer decides they want a different perspective, they can change the channel. But when it comes to online information sources, changing the channel isn't always an option. On Google, users who enter the same search terms will often get very different results based on their geography and browser histories. On Facebook, powerful personalization algorithms automatically provide users their own tailor-made streams of posts designed to be — in the words of a company spokesperson — *useful and relevant.*

While personalized information may sound innocuous or even advantageous in theory, in practice it creates a hall of mirrors in which millions of Americans are exposed almost exclusively to information and viewpoints that reflect what they already believe. In a 2018 presentation to Facebook executives, a group of employees warned about the dangers of the system they'd built. "Our algorithms exploit the human brain's attraction to divisiveness." Left unchecked, they explained, the system would feed users "more and more divisive content in an effort to gain user attention and increase time on the platform." Users might sign up for Facebook because they want to reconnect with long-lost friends, but over time they're sucked into a wormhole of informational affirmation. Those who lean right are pulled even deeper into a universe where climate change is a conspiracy, while those who lean left are ushered into a cosmos where all conservatives are racist. From the algorithm's perspective, it doesn't matter whether the posts it serves up are true. It only matters whether people click them.

More than half of American adults today get their news from Facebook, which in 2019 earned more than $70 billion by inserting ads into our feeds. Google earned more than twice that. Yet while the individualization of reality that powers these companies is great for their bottom lines, it's devastating for our democracy. After all, how can we debate one another's viewpoints if we don't even know they exist?

Because so many of our divisions these days are couched in political terms — liberals versus conservatives; left versus right — many people assume that the gravest threat facing American democracy is partisanship. If we could just "meet in the middle," many argue, we'd function better as a country. I disagree. Since 1920, Republicans and Democrats have cast nearly 2 billion votes for president, and in that entire time Republicans are ahead by just 0.3%. We've always been divided as a citizenry, indeed nearly evenly so, yet we've still managed to hold the country together. This suggests to me that partisanship is not the most dangerous threat we face.

Instead, I think the true danger is something more subtle yet far more corrosive: the calcification of certainty and the widespread belief that we needn't consider alternate perspectives because we already know the answers. We all think something different, and we're all convinced we're right. This is why media organizations like Fox News, MSNBC, Google, and Facebook are so dangerous. They are not agnostic brokers of information but certainty machines. Far from challenging us to think rationally, they discourage us from thinking at all. This invitation to complacency may feel comforting to us as individuals, but it's cancerous for a democratic society. It will be hard for our country to survive it.

Fortunately, there's hope. For even though many adults may have settled already on their conclusions about the world, there's another group of people that hasn't yet: children. And while modern media may have faltered in its purpose to help us think clearly, there's another place that still can: school. And, more specifically, math class.

Math Class: The Incubator of a Thoughtful Society

Mathematics is a powerful tool for exploring the questions that characterize real life. The math classroom is the perfect forum for students to reason about a range of social issues, and when they disagree, to do so with facts and respect. As the trustee of math, you can cultivate a new generation of critical thinkers, and in so doing act as a bulwark against the irrational backsliding that threatens our American experiment.

I didn't always think this. I didn't always recognize the role that we math educators can play in safeguarding self-governance. It was only when I attended the health care town hall meeting in 2009 that I realized the totality of our potential. As I sat on the basketball court on that August afternoon, I observed the screaming and finger-pointing around me and thought to myself, "If we could just have this conversation using seventh-grade probabilities, how much more productive would it be? Even if Congress won't discuss health care mathematically," I reasoned, "students can."

And as a math teacher, you're the one to show them how.

In this era of ideological rigidity and intellectual complacency, you can inspire a new archetype of mathematical citizen, a "Citizen Math" who moves through life in constant pursuit of a more refined understanding of the world around them. Someone who challenges convention and allows evidence to inform their opinions. Someone who welcomes opposing viewpoints as opportunities to hone their own. When such a person hears a cable news pundit criticize fast food companies for underpaying their employees, they don't immediately conclude that the government should increase the minimum wage. They withhold judgement until they weigh the upsides of an increased wage against the downside of employers possibly hiring fewer workers, an analysis powered by linear functions. When they read about an epidemic of opioid deaths, they don't reflexively blame patients or pharmaceutical companies. They consider the relationship between overmedication and opioid tolerance, a phenomenon modeled by exponential decay.

Of course, Citizen Math uses math to do more than *think* more clearly. They also use it to *live* more intentionally. When scrolling through social media, they might keep track of the ratio of substantive news stories to sensationalist clickbait and adjust their media consumption to balance being informed with not becoming jaded. When at a restaurant, they may order multiple appetizers instead of a single entrée to avoid diminishing returns. For such a person, math is a lens for viewing every dimension of reality, and the lens is always on. And should someone disagree with a conclusion they draw or a comment they make, Citizen Math doesn't react defensively. They simply respond, "I'll share with you my reasoning, and I'd like to hear yours."

Students have asked for generations why they're learning math and when they'll ever use it. This is unnecessary, even ironic. Math isn't some arbitrary collection of skills to memorize. It's a prism for looking at the world, for analyzing how it works and reimagining how it could. Math class needn't be something that students dread. It can be the setting for the most interesting conversations they'll ever have. *Are humans innovating faster that we can keep up with the consequences? Is there an upside to feeling sad? How much can you trust your memory, and is there a benefit to forgetting?* The world is full of fascinating questions. The math classroom is the ideal place to discuss them.

Still, as easy as it is to talk about a more expansive version of math class, actually creating it will require work. Isaac Newton observed that an object at rest will remain at rest unless acted upon by an outside force. For decades American math educatioan has operated largely on inertia. If we're to fulfill our potential as educators, we'll need to shift how we approach certain areas of our discipline. There are four areas in particular that I think we need to reevaluate:

1.   For much of our history, we've defined the purpose of learning math strictly as mastering procedures and understanding concepts. By maintaining this

narrow conception of a complete math education, we risk treating as "transformative" innovations which are really marginal improvements to longstanding practices. When we do this, we often believe that we're "revolutionizing" math instruction when we're just offering a slightly different version of the same experience that students have always received. If we're to expand the frontiers of math instruction, then we need to stop conflating superficial upgrades with fundamental change.

2. Students have long questioned the purpose of learning math. In an attempt to make math "real," teachers and curriculum developers often situate tasks in "real world" contexts. In most cases, though, these contexts merely serve as a prism for illustrating some underlying concept or skill. If we want to help students think critically about authentic issues around them, we need to differentiate between *learning math* and *applying math to learn about something else*; between using the world to look at math and using math to analyze the world.

3. Even when educators recognize the difference between *learning math* and *using math*, they offer many justifications for not exploring social issues in their classrooms. These include the assumption that these topics are better left to other teachers, that their students aren't ready for them, and that they won't be on the test. If math class is to prepare students to analyze the world around them, then we must give ourselves permission to prioritize the types of authentic activities that we've historically overlooked.

4. In recent years, educators, policy makers, philanthropists, and others have sought to use technology to "personalize" math instruction. While computer-driven personalized learning may play a helpful role in specific contexts, when taken too far it can undermine the social character of school. If math class is to act as an incubator of thoughtful social discourse, then we must approach the technologization of instruction carefully and demand that our classrooms remain settings for community-based learning experiences.

Since I view these four key areas as instrumental to our progress, the majority of this letter is dedicated to them.

I've also included brief examples between the chapters illustrating how mathematics can be used to explore different issues in the world: for instance, the fake discounts that retailers offer to lure customers (percents and proportions), and the possible advantages of having a bad day (positive and negative integers). The purpose of these mini-essays is three-fold. First, the phrase "real-world applications" gets tossed around a lot in math circles, but it isn't well defined. The vignettes are intended to concretize exactly what I mean when I refer to "applying math to the world." Second, by addressing a diversity of issues, the vignettes highlight the breadth of real-world topics that mathematics can illuminate and which we as educators can discuss with our students. And third, I hope they act as conversation starters in your own life. One of the main insights which I hope you carry from this letter is how mathematical reasoning can improve the quality of our discourse. To that end, I've included discussion prompts after each example. I hope they spark vibrant conversations between you and your friends...and offer a glimpse of what it means to be a Citizen Math.

I'm writing you this letter at the start of 2021, in the wake of what many Americans believe was one of our worst years yet. In many ways, though, I've been composing it ever since I got home from that disastrous health care town hall meeting a dozen years ago. That was the moment I realized the critical role that math educators can play in strengthening our democracy and restoring our commitment to reason. At the time I was working as a middle school math coach outside of Washington, DC. The morning after the debacle, I sat down at my desk and began writing a lesson about insurance markets. In it, students used probabilities and expected value to discuss insurance from the perspectives of both consumers and insurance companies. They analyzed the tension between the individual mandate and preexisting conditions and debated the pros and cons of the various policies that Congress was considering. Though I was deeply discouraged by the irrationality and vitriol that many adults exhibited in their debates, I was confident that students would analyze health insurance more rigorously and engage with one another more respectfully.

In the following months I wrote lessons on other topics, as well. I started a website to share the lessons with educators and named it Mathalicious (after my favorite rap group, Blackalicious). As Mathalicious grew, my colleagues and I developed activities on everything from climate change to government surveillance, pandemics to the evolution of video games. As former teachers ourselves, our goal was to help educators help students use math to analyze the world around them and to emerge from the classroom as more curious and reason-minded citizens.

Inspired by this vision, we eventually decided to change our name. The new name, Citizen Math, is inspired by what we as a people – students, teachers, and beyond – can become: beings who use math to clarify our understanding of the world and inform how we participate in it.

I've spent roughly fifteen years in American math education, or most of my adult life. I have tremendous respect for what this community does every day, and I feel a deep sense of kinship with those who teach math. At the same time, I believe that we have settled for a smaller mathematical experience than what students deserve, what the country needs, and what we are eminently capable of providing. This letter will at times offer a stinging critique of the status quo. I offer it for a simple reason: to communicate how powerful we are as a group and how much we can accomplish when we recalibrate our understanding of what it means to teach math. This is the optimism that motivates this letter. I feel privileged to share it with you.

As Americans, we're at an inflection point in our national experiment, and our prospects seem bleak. We shout but don't listen. We opine but don't reason. As the world grows more complex, we somehow emerge more certain. The consequences of this are dire. They may even be civilization-ending. But they're not inevitable. We can choose to redirect our democracy toward a more constructive trajectory and kindle a society committed to curiosity and respect. And mathematics can help. Mathematics is a tool that we humans have invented to explore the world around us and to think more creatively about it. The more the media hypnotizes us into a coma of braindead certainty, the more math class must pick up the slack. Math is a way of thinking, and you are the one we've entrusted to teach it.

In this season of unreason, you may be our last hope, our best bet, and our most precious national resource. Perhaps this sounds crazy. It's surely unorthodox. But I absolutely believe it. As a country, we deserve to discover a more rational version of ourselves. As a math educator, you are the perfect person to reveal it.

FAKE DISCOUNTS

Should retailers raise the price of items in order to put them on sale?

mathematics used: percents and proportions

E VERYONE loves a good deal. This is true of shoppers, and also of retailers. Retailers have long used coupons to lure customers to their stores, always with the promise of big savings, and often with tremendous success. Yet as ubiquitous as coupons have become in our shopping culture, they can be deceiving. For instance, imagine you're in the market for a new sweatshirt and come across the following offers. Without calculating anything — based only on your gut — which coupon do you expect represents the better deal?

Offer 1   Offer 2

If you're like most people, you might intuit that the second offer is better. After all, a discount of 70% is clearly superior to a discount of 20%. Yet when you actually calculate the final prices of the two sweatshirts, you find that they're exactly the same. After the discounts are applied, both sweatshirts cost $24. How is this possible?

The answer, of course, has to do with the starting price of the sweatshirts. In the first scenario, the advertised price of the sweatshirt is $30. This means that a coupon for 20% off represents a discount of 0.20($30) = $6 and a final price of $30 – $6 = $24. In the second scenario, the advertised price of the sweatshirt is $80. Here, a coupon for 70% off represents a discount of 0.70($80) = $56 and a final price of $80 – $56 = $24. Again, and contrary to many shoppers' intuition, the two offers are identical. Even though the second coupon allows customers to *save more*, that's only because the second sweatshirt *costs more* to begin with.

Or does it? Like a billboard ad, a coupon is just a form of marketing. Its purpose is to convince people to buy something. One of the most effective ways that retailers do this is by creating the *appearance* of savings; they inflate the price of an item in order to put it on sale, creating for customers the impression of having scored a great deal. Retailers have used this tactic for ages. The higher they raise the price, the bigger the discount they can offer, and the better the deal will seem

It came as quite a surprise, then, when in 2001 JCPenney announced that it was doing away with coupons. The company's new CEO, Ron Johnson, had previously worked at Apple, which is famously averse to discounts. Johnson reasoned that coupons were wasteful; they required buying ads in local newspapers and circulars, replacing in-store signage, and updating prices in computers. Instead of relying on coupons to draw shoppers to its stores, JCPenney would switch to a system of everyday low prices which it called "Fair and Square." Under Fair and Square, the average list price of an item at JCPenney was 40% lower than before. Thanks to JCPenney's new policy, customers no longer needed to wait for the store to put some of their favorite items on sale. Now shoppers could save on all of their favorite items automatically, and without having to snip coupons from the paper. So how did shoppers react to Fair and Square? Now that prices were no longer inflated artificially, surely they must have been thrilled, right?

Wrong. Customers hated JCPenney's new pricing and fled the store in droves. Within a year of the transition, sales at some stores fell by 30%. The company posted a net loss of almost $1 billion and its stock price tanked. Why? If Fair and Square actually offered shoppers a better deal rather than simply the appearance of one, why did they dislike it so much?

To understand customers' reactions, it's helpful to consider how much an item under Fair and Square would have cost before the change. In other words, rather than focus on how much customers were paying under the new system, we can calculate how much *they thought they were losing* by no longer getting a discount. For example, under Fair and Square a pair of aviator sunglasses cost $75. Again, this price is 40% lower than what it was before. So what must the price have been in the original couponing era…and how much would a coupon have been worth?

Saying that an item costs 40% less than the original price is equivalent to saying that it costs 60% of the original price. We can use this insight to create a diagram to determine the pre-coupon price of the sunglasses. If $75 represents 60% of the original price — or put another way, if $75 represents *six tenths* of the original price — then *one tenth* of the original price must be $75 ÷ 6 = $12.50. This implies that the original price of the sunglasses was $12.50 · 10 = $125.

Fair & Square 60%						Original 100%			
$12.50	$12.50	$12.50	$12.50	$12.50	$12.50	$12.50	$12.50	$12.50	$12.50

$75 $125

From JCPenney's perspective, a customer was paying $75 for the glasses. But from many customers' perspectives, they were losing out on $50 worth of savings. Under the couponing scheme, the only time a customer would have received the glasses for $75 was when the company put them on sale; otherwise they would have paid $125. Under Fair and Square, the customer always got the lower price.

Yet even though shoppers were better off under the new system, many felt like they were doing worse. When a backpack that had previously been listed at the artificial price of $100 was now offered at the more accurate $60, customers didn't celebrate its everyday low price; instead, they bemoaned the loss of the $40 discount. It's as though by not seeing the discount taking place, shoppers assumed it didn't exist. While visiting a mall in Cincinnati, a mother explained her decision to abandon JCPenney. "I wasn't getting the deals I used to get," she said confidently, "with the coupons in the mail."

Less than two years after launching Fair and Square, JCPenney cancelled its policy of everyday low prices, fired its CEO, and reinstated coupons... including the fake prices that allowed them. In fact, some stores reverted to the old prices so quickly that they didn't have time to print new labels; they simply put stickers with the higher prices over the lower Fair and Square ones. For brick-and-mortar stores like JCPenney and Michaels, and for online retailers such as Blair and Vistaprint, this reliance on artificial discounts is central to their business. Marketers have been studying consumer behavior for years, and they know that people often care less about how much they spend than about how much they think they save. When we find a coupon offering a big discount, we pride ourselves for being savvy shoppers, though in many cases we're being played.

In recent years, consumer advocates have begun to push back against what they see as fraudulent retailer behavior. Under California law, retailers who describe an item as being "on sale" can only include the previous price if it truly was the prevailing market price within three months of the advertisement. In 2016, the attorney for the city of Los Angeles sued JCPenney, Kohl's, Sears, and Macy's for deceptive pricing. "Customers have the right to be told the truth about the prices they're paying," Mike Feuer explained, "and to know if a bargain is really a bargain."

On one hand, this seems fair; since a store that advertises a discount is essentially promising customers that they're saving money, it seems reasonable to require that the promise be true. On the other hand, when JCPenney took the high road and replaced fake prices with accurate ones, customers abandoned its stores. Retailers are stuck between a rock and a hard place: between the requirement to be honest...and our desire to be fooled.

Discussion Questions

- If you were a customer shopping for a new sweatshirt, which of the following offers would you find the most appealing: $24 with no discount; $40 with a 40% discount; or $240 with a 90% discount?

- If you were the manager of a store (or the CEO of a major retailer), what factors would you consider when deciding whether or not to offer discounts?

- Do you think retailers should be allowed to artificially raise the prices of items in order to put them on sale?

PART TWO

THE NEW OLD THINGS

N a 2012 survey, 44% of middle school students said they'd rather take out the garbage than do their math homework. To millions of children, learning math isn't just a chore. It's worse. This isn't a new phenomenon. I read once that when Pythagoras started teaching math more than two thousand years ago, he had to pay his students to attend class. Many students today view math as little more than a collection of random skills to memorize and regurgitate, a tool whose only purpose is to answer questions that only textbooks would ask: *What's the square root of q^9? How many marbles fit in a jar? What time will the train reach the station?*

The eye-rolling disdain that students feel for math is not an indication that teachers haven't tried to provide a more meaningful and fulfilling learning experience. Math educators have been trying for decades to convince students that math is worth learning. In 1920, for instance, the National Council of Teachers of Mathematics was founded to professionalize math instruction. Since then, educators from across the country have gathered each year for its annual conference to learn new teaching strategies and attend workshops on topics such as "Empowering Algebraic Thinkers" and "Strategies to Spark Engagement." They've purchased new curricula and adopted digital technologies. They've attended seminars on growth mindsets, rethought homework policies, and double-blocked classes districtwide. And yet for all the energy that math educators have expended to transform what happens in their classrooms —

and despite whatever success teachers might have experienced — students continue to ask the same questions that their parents asked and their parents before them: *Why are we learning math and when will we use it?*

Why is this happening? If educators have worked so hard for so long to improve math instruction, why do students remain so skeptical about it? I think the reason is simple. For all the improvements that we as an educational community have made in how we *present* mathematics, the way we *define* mathematics has remained more or less unchanged. For generations we have viewed the purpose of our profession as helping students master mathematical procedures, understand mathematical concepts, and develop strategies for solving and discussing mathematical problems. These are the components that we've historically defined as constituting a "complete" math experience. And yet when students ask why they're learning math, what they're asking is why they need procedures, concepts, and problem-solving strategies in the first place. While teachers are focused on helping students *learn math*, students are asking when they'll ever *use math*. This is not a question that we've answered... which explains why we continue to hear it.

If students are to react to math differently than they historically have, then we as educators must expand our understanding of what math is and what it means to teach it. We haven't done this yet. Instead, our strategy for improving math instruction has historically been limited to modifying the same underlying experience that we've always provided. Some of the steps that we've taken as a community have been helpful, and many modern approaches are worth incorporating. Still, if all we do is iterate on what we've always done, then the only place we'll get is where we've always been.

The Math Wars: Big Battle, Small Field

One of the clearest examples of the traditionalism of American math instruction can be found in a debate that's raged since the mid 20th century. The disagreement is known as the Math Wars. It pits old-school proceduralists against new-school conceptualists, and it's focused on the optimal balance between procedural fluency and conceptual understanding.

Those in the proceduralist camp believe that for students to develop a solid mathematical foundation, they must begin by mastering skills and developing fluency. When introducing a topic like subtracting negative integers or solving linear equations, educators in the proceduralist camp typically begin by explaining the steps involved in solving a problem, then assigning students numerous practice problems to solve on their own. These are the types of activities commonly found in workbooks and on test prep websites, and in a classroom they may be launched with an assignment like "Do 1–35, odd."

Conceptualists, on the other hand, take a different approach. Instead of leading with automaticity, reform-minded educators believe that students must start by exploring the meaning behind mathematical concepts. Rather than tell students how to solve a certain kind of problem, conceptualist teachers will often assign a task with no clear solution method, such as a word problem grounded in some ostensibly "real world" scenario.

Topic	Procedural Fluency	Conceptual Understanding
Subtracting Negative Integers	simplify the following: 500 – (-200)	A hiker starts at the beginning of a trail which is 200 feet below sea level. He hikes to a location that's 500 feet above sea level. What is the total vertical distance that the hiker hiked, and how did you arrive at your answer?
Writing & Solving Equations	solve for x: 3x + 2 = 17	Johnny has two more than three times as many pencils as Debbie has. If Johnny has 17 pencils, how many pencils does Debbie have? Use a diagram to represent your solution.

Many educators have strong opinions about which approach is better, and for good reason: each has its advantages. Fans of proceduralism argue that rote practice ensures that students develop the mathematical muscle memory that they'll need in subsequent courses. Not only that, but since teachers are required to cover many topics in a given year — 28 standards in eighth grade alone — they reason that a mechanical approach is the only realistic way to do it. Critics of proceduralism respond that it relies too heavily on memorization and effectively guarantees that students will forget much of what they're taught. And since proceduralist instruction often involves tricks like "minus minus plus," conceptualists argue that it primes students to view mathematics unfairly as an arbitrary rulebook that fell from the sky. ("And God said unto Eve, 'Eat thou not of the apple. And also, subtracting a negative means adding a positive.'") Instead of leading with procedures, reformists argue that a more conceptual approach helps students develop and retain an intuitive understanding of math, and that activities like word problems develop students into flexible problem solvers who can justify their solutions instead of operating as rote robots. Of course, proceduralists have a reply. "Allowing kids to discover math on their own sounds good," they say. "But it leaves them without fluency, takes too much class time, and requires complex pedagogical skills that many teachers lack." And so on goes the debate.

The tug-of-war between proceduralists and conceptualists has raged for the better part of a century. In the first half of the 1900s, most American math textbooks emphasized mechanical drill. During the space race with the Soviets in the 1960s, educators shifted towards the flexible problem-solving of conceptualism. Battle lines shifted back towards proceduralism a decade later, until the conceptualists regained the upper hand with the publication of the Common Core Standards and their emphasis on mathematical reasoning.

Given the intense characterization of the debate — a math *war* — an outside observer might conclude that students in different eras must have received very different experiences and that a child in a traditionalist classroom will learn math completely differently than one in a reformist environment. In fact, they don't. For all the talk of "battle lines" dividing traditionalists and reformers, their differences are fairly minor. Proceduralists agree that students need to understand mathematical concepts, and traditionalist textbooks include plenty of word problems. Conceptualists agree that students must develop procedural fluency, and their resources involve rote practice. The two camps agree on the need for both automaticity and understanding; they simply disagree on which to start with and how much time to spend on each. That's it. In the history of American math education, that's been our biggest debate. It isn't a philosophical dispute over the ultimate destination of math instruction. It's merely a squabble over the route.

So why does this matter?

By treating as an existential crisis what is in fact a tactical difference, the Math Wars reveal just how much even the most extreme math partisans have in common. As a community, we've disagreed passionately about how to best blend procedures and concepts, but we've agreed entirely that *these are the ingredients to be blended.* As a result, whenever we try to improve how students experience math, we limit our focus to approaches that are designed for fluency and understanding, neither of which addresses students' perception of math as irrelevant. This perpetuates a maddening cycle. Regardless of what era they've been in — traditional or reform — students have always questioned the value of mathematical skills and concepts. And yet our reaction as a teaching community has historically been to say, "Our kids dislike math and perform poorly in it. You know what we need? Better ways to teach procedures and concepts!" And so we adopt new strategies and buy new products. And we convince ourselves that we've finally revolutionized math instruction. And yet very little changes, for all we've really done is to create a slightly different version of the same traditional experience.

To demonstrate what I mean, let me share with you three examples of recent innovations which math educators and others have heralded as "transformative," but which are in fact superficial upgrades to our traditional approach. Each example represents an improvement over what came before it. Each offers something better. But none offers anything fundamentally different. The following innovations all improve the *way* that we present math instruction, but they don't change at all what our instruction is *for*.

Innovation 1: Khan Academy — Rote Lectures You Can Rewind

Ten years ago, the education world began to light up with stories about an online library of instructional videos and practice exercises. The site, Khan Academy, was founded by former hedge fund analyst Sal Khan, who a few years earlier had begun remotely tutoring his middle school cousin in math. As more family members joined their tutorials, Khan began recording his lectures with a digital tablet and screen-capture software and posting his videos on YouTube. By 2009, his eponymous Khan Academy was attracting more than 200,000 visitors each month. By 2020, his videos had been viewed nearly 2 billion times by learners around the world, an incredible accomplishment for someone who started with no formal teaching experience and a few hundred dollars' worth of technology from Best Buy.

Today, many people view Khan Academy as a transformative invention for teaching math. A Houston Public Media story heard on NPR suggested that Khan was "revolutionizing online education." An article in Forbes described how Khan Academy was "blowing up traditional models" of school and represented a "completely new way to teach children math." *TIME* named Khan one of its 100 most influential people on the planet, while *Businessweek* went so far as to anoint him the "Messiah of Math." Across the country, schools and districts have adopted Khan Academy videos as a core instructional resource. The state of Idaho even launched a pilot to incorporate the resource statewide.

Yet for all the talk of Khan Academy representing a "completely new way to teach," its style of instruction is entirely familiar. When you watch the videos that Khan has created, you quickly see that the type of instruction he offers is identical to what students have seen for years. For instance, consider how algebra teachers have long approached the process for solving linear equations. Take the problem $20 - 7x = 6x - 6$. In many classrooms, a teacher begins by instructing students to subtract 20 from both sides of the equation (leaving $-7x = 6x - 26$). Next, they tell students to subtract 6x from both sides (leaving $-13x = -26$). Finally, they tell students to divide both sides by -13 (revealing the solution, $x = 2$). This is exactly how teachers have taught this skill for centuries.

So what does the process sound like on Khan Academy?

Solving Linear Equations, Khan Academy

"So to get the 20 out of the way from the left-hand side, let's subtract it from the left-hand side. But this is an equation. Anything you do to the left-hand side you also have to do to the right-hand side. So I subtracted 20 from the left. Let me also subtract 20 from the right."

As the transcript makes clear, the style of teaching that students receive on Khan Academy is identical to what they receive in proceduralist classrooms. The only difference is that it happens online. In addition to explanatory videos, Khan Academy also offers assessments like multiple choice questions and fill-in-the-blanks. Yet these too are identical to what students find in workbooks and homework packets; the main improvement is that they're digital. Khan Academy has been credited with revolutionizing how students learn math. In reality, there's nothing revolutionary about it. This shouldn't come as a surprise. In a 2011 interview, Khan described the process he used when preparing his lessons. Before recording a video, he would reference Wikipedia, the Internet, his library, and even "Idiot's Guide" books. In other words, the educational resource that many were heralding as one of the most transformative in human history basically comes down to a guy copying textbooks into YouTube.

There's nothing wrong with this. Khan Academy is a helpful resource. It's great for kids in areas who don't have access to textbooks. It's great for students who need help with their homework or extra practice before a test. Even if the words that Sal Khan is saying aren't new, the fact that he's saying them online allows viewers to listen to them over and over, which is critical for kids who digest math more slowly and need more time to learn it. Khan once described how prison inmates sometimes send letters to his staff thanking them for reinvigorating their passion for learning and giving them hope in a demoralizing environment. That's awesome. I like Khan Academy. I've even used it myself when I forgot how to multiply matrices and visited the site for a refresher. Khan Academy is valuable. But while Sal Khan may have transformed how students access math instruction, the instruction itself is the same as ever. Indeed, it's exactly this familiarity that's responsible for Khan Academy's popularity. Contrary to what many believe, the fact that so many people adopted the service so quickly is not an indication that Khan Academy is transformative, but evidence that it's not. The service does not provide users with a different experience of math. It provides exactly the experience that millions have come to expect: test prep and homework help. Khan Academy is rote proceduralism, YouTube-ified. As a tool for strengthening mathematical muscle memory, its library of videos and practice exercises is great. But when we as educators adopt Khan Academy with the expectation that it will "revolutionize" how students learn, we reveal just how traditional our conception remains about what mathematics is and what it means to teach it.

Innovation 2: EngageNY and Illustrative Math — Same Problems, Lower Price

One of the main goals of the 2010 Common Core Standards was to encourage a shift from emphasizing procedures and automaticity to emphasizing concepts and understanding. Like nutritional guidelines, learning standards outline the information that students need to digest each year. It's the curriculum, meanwhile, that's the meal. While standards tell educators what to teach, the curriculum is what they use to do it.

After the Common Core was released, many textbook publishers responded by slapping stickers on old materials assuring that they were properly aligned. Educators saw through this false marketing. It took a few years, though, for curriculum developers to publish materials that truly reflected the new standards. One of the first was a curriculum called EngageNY. This was followed a few years later by another from Illustrative Mathematics (IM). Desperate to satisfy the Common Core, schools and districts across the country quickly adopted these resources. When EdReports, a non-profit organization that reviews instructional materials, evaluated the EngageNY and Illustrative Math curriculums, it gave them both high marks. In fact, it awarded Illustrative Math's middle school curriculum the highest possible score in every evaluation category. According to EdReports, Illustrative Math isn't just good. It's perfect.

And yet like Khan Academy, it's very traditional. Take the topic from before: solving linear equations. To introduce this, a textbook published in 1979 called *Mathematics in Our World* asked, "A stagecoach driver has $32 and saves $4 per month. In how many months will the driver have $100?" To anyone who's studied algebra, this type of word problem will look familiar. So what kinds of problems do EngageNY and Illustrative Math pose to address this topic?

EngageNY	Illustrative Mathematics
The cost of a babysitting service on a cruise is $10 for the first hour and $12 for each additional hour. If the total cost of babysitting baby Aaron was $58, for how many hours was Aaron at the sitter?	*Kiran is trying to save $144 to buy a new guitar. He has $34 and is going to save $10 a week from money he earns mowing lawns. How many weeks it will take him to have enough money to buy the guitar?*

The tasks that students find in the EngageNY and Illustrative Math curriculums today are almost identical to those that they found in textbooks forty years ago. The only change that the authors made was to swap the context from driving a stagecoach to doing chores. This strategy of updating old word problems isn't limited to middle school. Consider how the curriculum authors address the high school topic of exponential growth.

EngageNY	Illustrative Mathematics
An equipment rental company charges a different late fee each day. On day 1, the penalty is $0.01. On day 2, the penalty is $0.02. On day 3, the penalty is $0.04, and so on. What will the penalty be on day 15?	*A purse contains 1 penny today. Tomorrow it will magically turn into 2 pennies. The next day it will turn into 4 pennies, doubling each day. How many pennies will be in the purse after 30 days?*

Math teachers have been using some version of this doubling problem to contextualize exponential growth for ages. A riddle from the year 1256 asks, "A chessboard has 1 grain of wheat on the first square, 2 grains on the second square, 4 grains on the third, and so on. If a chessboard has 64 squares, how many grains will be on the final square?" Nearly 800 years later, all EngageNY and Illustrative Mathematics did was to replace wheat grains with coins.

The fact that these resources aren't especially innovative is not an argument against using them. On the contrary, if I were a curriculum coordinator for a school district, I'd likely adopt one of them. Math teachers are required to address a specific set of skills and concepts each year, and EngageNY and Illustrative Math reliably support them in doing this.

Illustrative Math is especially helpful. One of the most valuable contributions it offers is fewer tasks per day. Math teachers often feel pressured to cram as many problems as possible into a class period. While this "drill and kill" strategy keeps students busy, it can rob them of the time they need to think deeply about the work they're doing and reflect on mathematical meaning. By reducing the number of problems that educators are obliged to teach, Illustrative Math gives students breathing room to explore the math in more depth and time to come up with novel strategies and discuss them with their peers. Not only that, but Illustrative Math also includes a range of support resources to ensure that teachers are successful, from lesson guides with intuitive mathematical explanations and teacher tips to supports for English language learners. The curriculum even includes online digital simulations to help students visualize mathematical ideas.

And to top it off, both Illustrative Math and EngageNY offer their benefits for free. Because each resource was published under a non-commercial Creative Commons license, they cost educators nothing to use. For generations schools and districts have spent tens of thousands of dollars each year on textbooks and other materials. In making their products free, EngageNY and Illustrative Math have upended the economics of curriculum.

But the actual takeaways that students gain from them are the same as ever. One of the reasons that students think math class is pointless is its historical reliance on made-up word problems about silly situations. When you strip away the teacher guides and online interactives and open licenses, you find that EngageNY and Illustrative Math offer the familiar old-school conceptualism, just at a lower price.

They ask students to do exactly what they've being doing since (literally) the Middle Ages. When EdReports concludes that these curriculums "meet expectations," then, it doesn't mean that the resources are transformative. It simply means that they satisfy the expectations that we've come to accept about the purpose of math education. And yet as students have made clear for years, these expectations were never enough.

Innovation 3: Makeover Math — Math Class Gets Makeup

In a 2010 TED talk entitled "Math Class Needs a Makeover," a high school teacher in California proposed a fix for the off-putting word problems that have long alienated math students. Dan Meyer shared with his audience an activity from a popular textbook, then explained the shortcomings he saw. The task showed a diagram of an octagonal water tank, which the accompanying text said was being filled with water. "The base octagon has side length of 11.9 cm," the textbook authors specified. "The lateral edge of the water tank is 36 cm. If you pour water into the tank at a rate of 1.8 oz./sec., how long will it take to fill the tank?"

According to Meyer, the task's main flaw was that it included all of the information that students would need to answer the question. By revealing upfront the dimensions of the tank and the flow rate of the water, the textbook authors had turned what could have been a valuable challenge into a paint-by-numbers process that only required students to plug values into a formula. The activity would have been more meaningful, Meyer explained, had students been required to determine on their own what information they'd need. Not only would this be more intellectually demanding, it would also be more fun.

Meyer then revealed his upgraded version of the task: a video of himself standing in the backyard filling a tank with a hose. The video didn't include numbers. It didn't even specify a question. It simply introduced a situation and let students take it from there. Meyer calls his multimedia-driven approach to task redevelopment "Three Act Math." In Act One, the teacher uses a video, photograph, or digital simulation to introduce a scenario and spark student interest. In Act Two, students request information and attempt a solution. In Act Three, the teacher reveals the answer. This, Meyer explained to his audience, is how math tasks should be designed.

"So now we have the real deal," he beamed. "Students are looking at their watches, rolling their eyes, and they're all wondering at some point or another, 'Man, how long is it going to take to fill up?' That's how you know you've baited the hook!"

In the years since his presentation, Meyer has become one of the most well-known figures in American math education. By 2020, his talk had been viewed almost 3 million times. More than 30,000 educators subscribe to his blog, and 80,000 people follow him on Twitter. At national conferences, teachers crowd shoulder-to-shoulder to hear Meyer discuss his approach to mathematical storytelling, the narrative arc of which he likens to dramatic filmmaking. Textbook publishers have hired Meyer to breathe life into their lessons, and scores of teachers have launched their own Three Act-inspired initiatives. In a 2015 article entitled "The Man Who Will Save Math," the *New Republic* described Meyer as the "most famous math educator in America," presenting him as a sort of curricular apostle who travels the country "sharing his gospel."

This is curious. Because for all the religious allegory, the vision of math class that Dan Meyer is espousing is entirely familiar. To improve a task in which students calculate how many meatballs fit in a pot, Meyer photographed himself cooking at a stove. To enliven one in which students estimate how many pennies fit in a circle, he filmed himself arranging coins on a carpet. By using videos and other technologies to deconstruct and then reconstruct existing tasks, Meyer provides teachers with a better way to pose mathematical questions. The questions themselves, however, remain unchanged: *How many pennies fit in a circle? How many meatballs fit in a pot?*

To be sure, the multimedia activities that Dan Meyer has created are superior to the original textbook versions. Because words are replaced with visuals, Meyer's remakes are more accessible to students who don't read well or who struggle with English. By organizing problem-solving into discrete stages and withholding information until it's needed, his Three Act problems keep students engaged without being overwhelmed. Many students think of doing math as a solitary pursuit. By having students discuss their answers before revealing the actual solution – *I expect it'll take eight minutes to fill up the water tank! No, I expect it'll take eight and a half!* – teachers who use his tasks create environments that are livelier and more collaborative than many people expect from a math classroom. Not only that, but by prioritizing estimation over precision and reasoning over regimentation, Meyer's narrative-based approach to task redevelopment can help erode the concern that many students have about getting the wrong answer. In my opinion, the work that Meyer (and others) are doing represents one of the most valuable contributions to math education in years. Not only is it pedagogically thoughtful, it's deeply empathetic. Many kids are scared of math. Meyer's activities can make learning it more fun.

But they can't address students' deeper questions about the value of learning math. The improvements that Meyer and others like him are making are almost entirely surface-level. They improve how traditional problems are framed, but they don't change what the problems are. Still, this has not stopped teachers from adopting the tasks in the hope that they'll transform their classrooms or concluding that, if we as a community are to convince students that math is worth learning, all we need to do is give centuries-old word problems a multimedia "makeover." This is nonsensical. Using video cameras and digital simulations to remake traditional tasks can improve how students engage with math, but it does nothing to change what they're engaging with. Students have been solving problems involving water tanks, penny circles, and pots full of meatballs for ages, and many have concluded that math class is pointless. Remaking these tasks with a GoPro can make learning math more engaging. But it doesn't make it fundamentally different.

New Versions of the Old Thing

Given the skepticism that students feel about math, it's understandable when teachers are eager to try something new. And yet many of the resources that educators are adopting — even proclaiming as "transformative" — aren't new at all. They're simply the latest iterations on an age-old experience, the most recent ways to do what we've always done. This isn't unique to the resources we've explored. It's part of a larger phenomenon, from using video games for students to "zap" their times tables to installing iPad apps for them to share their work on word problems. Even after decades of such innovations, students are still asking the same question as ever: *When will we ever use this?* The problem isn't with the resources themselves. It's with our habit of confusing marginal improvement for fundamental change.

When we confuse iteration for revolution, the only "revolution" we achieve is that of the wheel: spinning around in circles and returning right back to where we started. The approach to math instruction that we've historically prioritized isn't bad. It's just incomplete. For years we've defined a comprehensive math education as consisting of procedural fluency, conceptual understanding, and mathematical problem solving. These are great and worthy components, but there's another that we've missed. Mathematics is larger than we've traditionally envisioned.

As math educators, we have an opportunity to help students think critically about important issues in the world and to emerge from our classrooms as more curious participants in society. If we're to accomplish this potential and inspire a new generation of Citizens Math, then it isn't enough to simply to ask the old questions differently. We also have to ask new questions.

INCOME, RENT, AND HOMELESSNESS

Should towns and cities recruit high-paying employers?

mathematics used: scatterplots and linear regressions

I N September 2017, the internet giant Amazon announced that it needed a second headquarters. Almost immediately, cities across the United States began working on pitches to become the home of the so-called "HQ2." While most of the proposals focused on practical matters like infrastructure and tax incentives, others bordered on shameless flattery. In New York City, local leaders illuminated the Empire State Building in Amazon's signature orange. In Tucson, Arizona, they sent a 21-foot tall cactus to Amazon's headquarters in Seattle. A restaurant in Pittsburgh offered to give every would-be Amazon employee a free sandwich, while a town in Georgia went so far as to promise to change its name from Stonecrest to Amazon.

As over-the-top as some of the pitches may have seemed, civic leaders had good reasons for recruiting Amazon. Amazon is one of the most successful companies in the world, and its new headquarters promised 50,000 new jobs. Many of these would pay more than $100,000 per year, nearly three times America's median annual income. To cities and towns hoping to expand their tax bases and improve their economies, HQ2 offered clear upsides.

However, might the project have had downsides, as well? For all the benefits that the headquarters offered, might it also have come with some costs?

To understand the impact that a project like HQ2 can have on its new home, it's helpful to consider the recent history of Amazon's original home, Seattle, Washington. In recent years, Seattle has become one of the fastest-growing cities in the country, thanks in large part to its collection of high-tech employers. At the same time, it's also become one of the most expensive cities in which to live. The following graphs show how the median annual household income and the median annual rent in Seattle rose in the decade between 2010 and 2019.

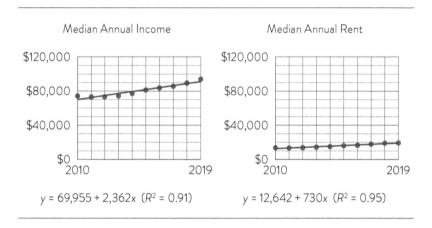

Median Annual Income

$$y = 69{,}955 + 2{,}362x \ (R^2 = 0.91)$$

Median Annual Rent

$$y = 12{,}642 + 730x \ (R^2 = 0.95)$$

After 2010, Seattle's median annual income rose significantly. As the trendline on the left indicates, the typical household saw its income rise by roughly $2,300 each year. As incomes rose, so did rents. Between 2010 and 2019, the median annual rent rose by almost $730 each year. Of course, this is exactly what many people might expect; as a city becomes more popular and its residents become wealthier, its housing becomes more expensive.

That said, we have to be careful about assuming that rents in Seattle rose *because* incomes rose. As intuitive as this may seem — the wealthier residents are, the more expensive a city becomes — it's possible that these two factors are unrelated. For instance, maybe rents rose because a flood destroyed a neighborhood, reducing the housing supply and causing landlords elsewhere in town to raise their rates. Or maybe the government raised property taxes and building owners passed the costs on to tenants. There are lots of reasons why rents might go up that have nothing to do with income.

When we directly compare the median annual rent and median household income in Seattle between 2010 and 2019, though, we see that they do appear very closely related. According to the R^2 value of the trendline (a number which mathematicians use to describe the strength of a relationship), 98% of the variation in rent can be explained by the linear model relating it to income. And

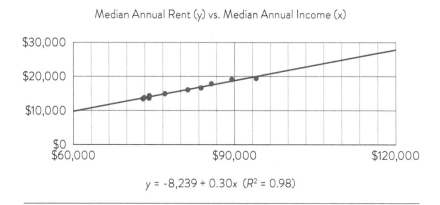

Median Annual Rent (y) vs. Median Annual Income (x)

$$y = -8,239 + 0.30x \quad (R^2 = 0.98)$$

according to the slope of the trendline, for every dollar that the median income rose, median rent rose by $0.30. In other words, roughly 30% of the additional income that the typical household earned over the decade went towards increased housing costs. That's a lot. But it's not everything. It still leaves 70%, which suggests that even as Seattle became a more and more expensive place to live, the typical household there was still left better off financially.

However, this wasn't true for everyone. For while Seattle's annual income and rent each rose over time, so did something else: its homeless population. Below, the graph on the left shows how point-in-time homelessness (the number of people experiencing homelessness at any given moment) increased over the decade. The graph on the right shows how the homeless population increased as the median annual rent increased.

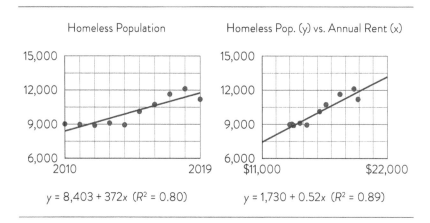

Homeless Population

$$y = 8,403 + 372x \quad (R^2 = 0.80)$$

Homeless Pop. (y) vs. Annual Rent (x)

$$y = 1,730 + 0.52x \quad (R^2 = 0.89)$$

On average, point-in-time homelessness in Seattle rose by 372 people each year. While some years did see a decline in the homeless population, the overall trend was upwards. According to the R^2 value of the trendline, roughly 89% of the variation in homelessness could be attributed to the linear model; this suggests a strong relationship between homelessness and rent. According to the slope of the trendline, for every dollar that the median annual rent increased, another 0.52 Seattle residents experienced homelessness at some point in the year. Put another way, for every $2 that annual housing costs went up, one more person lost their home.

As is often the case with mathematics, the graphs relating income, rent, and homelessness don't tell the whole story. But they do tell *a* story, and an important one. Between 2010 and 2019, Seattle's median annual income rose significantly, in large part because of an influx of high-tech workers earning high-dollar salaries. As incomes rose, so did rents. And as rents rose, so did homelessness. At first glance this seems like a paradox; if the typical Seattle household earned so much more money over time, why did so many more people become homeless? The answer is simple: not everyone is *typical*. While workers at high-tech employers like Amazon and Microsoft may have seen their incomes go up, many others didn't. These included teachers, restaurant workers, and Postal Service letter carriers. As Seattle became a more and more expensive place to live, they found it harder and harder to live there, and many were eventually priced out of their homes.

This story is not unique to Seattle. New York City, Los Angeles, and other parts of the United States have in recent years seen similar increases in income, rent, and homelessness. It's a tricky situation. On one hand, it makes sense that local officials and business leaders would want high-paying employers such as Amazon to move to their areas; they can yield tremendous economic benefits. On the other hand, the greater the benefits are to some residents, the higher the costs may be to others. So what's a city to do? There's no easy answer. What's clear, though, is that when evaluating a project like HQ2, localities need to consider more than just the promised gains. They must also consider the possible costs, however unintended they may be.

Discussion Questions

- In addition to higher incomes, rents, and homelessness, what might be some other consequences (both positive and negative) of a high-paying employer moving to a new area?

- Cities and towns have long offered incentives like new roads and tax breaks to attract high-paying companies to relocate to their areas. In recent years, they've also begun to offer incentives to highly-paid individuals to work remotely, as well. These can include relocation payments and even a free bike. What do you think of this idea?

- When an influx of high-paying jobs causes rents to go up, do you think anyone should be responsible for ensuring that the area remains affordable for existing residents? If so, whose responsibility do you think this should be: the local government, the company, charities, or someone else?

PART THREE

MATH AS A TELESCOPE

As we discussed, for the past century, American math education has defined the purpose of math instruction as helping students develop procedural fluency and conceptual understanding. When we prioritize procedures and concepts, we treat mathematics as something to look *at*. However, mathematics has another aspect that we tend to overlook: It's also something to look *with*. For most of our history, we've treated mathematics primarily as something to learn about. But it's also a tool that we can use to learn *about something else*: something external to math, something real in the world.

When I was a classroom teacher and instructional coach, I didn't think about mathematics as having these two separate parts to its nature. This distinction only crystalized for me a few years ago during a trip to Italy. I was in Florence for a friend's wedding. The day before the ceremony I visited the Galileo Museum, a four-story collection of the astronomer's tool and gadgets: the charts, compasses, and sundials that Galileo used to explore the night sky. The centerpiece, of course, was Galileo's telescopes. From finger-sized prisms encased in wood to meter-long cylinders of glass and steel, each telescope was a work of art. The polished metal. The precision of their dials and the curvature of their mirrors. As I stood gazing at one example after another, I thought, "These devices are beautiful."

And yet as elegant as telescopes are, astronomers don't spend years mastering how they work because they want to look *at* them. They do it because they want to look *with* them. Telescopes are powerful prisms that allow us to explore the reality around us.

Mathematics is the same. As a standalone discipline, mathematics is worth studying. Just as it's helpful to understand the inner workings of a telescope, it's valuable to study the inner workings of math. At the same time, if we're to become a more reason-minded society, it's necessary that we also apply math to real life. When students use probabilities to explore the tension between pre-existing conditions and the individual mandate, they emerge better able to discuss insurance reform. When students use surface area and volume to analyze disposable water bottles, they discover that while small bottles use less plastic in total, they use more plastic per ounce of water…and emerge more insightful about waste and recycling. Just as Galileo used his telescopes to observe the skies above us, we can use mathematics to explore the world around us, from issues of public policy to the curiosities of everyday life. When educators provide students with opportunities to apply math to real life, those students don't just become more complete mathematicians. They also become more thoughtful and curious citizens.

Looking At Math

To better understand what I mean by "looking at math" versus "looking with math," let's consider the types of tasks that students typically encounter in math class. For instance, imagine a high school teacher is teaching a unit on parabolas and quadratics. What types of activities do you expect they'd assign?

One common type of activity is referred to as "naked numbers" or "drill and kill." When it comes to quadratics, students might be given an equation and asked to manipulate it algebraically.

"Naked Numbers"

general form of quadratic function: $f(x) = ax^2 + bx + c$
formula for x-coordinate of vertex: $x = -b/(2a)$

What is the y-coordinate of the vertex of $f(x) = -16x^2 + 144x + 160?$

Tasks like these usually involve a predefined set of procedures which students are expected to memorize and follow. First, students use the vertex formula to find the *x*-coordinate of the vertex: $x = -b/(2a) = -144/(2 \cdot -16) = -144/(-32) = 4.5$.

Next, students plug this value into the function to determine the corresponding y-coordinate: $f(4.5) = -16(4.5)^2 + 144(4.5) + 160 = 484$, which is the desired answer. The purpose of this exercise is for students to develop fluency with quadratic functions. Put another way, teachers and curriculum developers intend the task as a way for students to look at mathematical procedures.

Another type of activity that teachers are likely to use during a unit on quadratics and parabolas is word problems involving some ostensibly "real-world" context. An activity in EngageNY's Algebra 1 curriculum asks:

Word Problem: Tennis Balls

A science class designed a ball launcher and tested it by shooting a tennis ball straight up from the top of a 15-story building. They determined that the motion of the ball could be described by the function $h(t) = -16t^2 + 144t + 160$, where t represents the time the ball is in the air and $h(t)$ represents the height, in feet, of the ball above the ground at time t. What is the maximum height of the ball?

Mathematically, the work that students do in this problem is the same as in the naked numbers task. The main difference is that because the word problem is situated in a context, students can relate the function's key features to something familiar. If students draw a parabola of the ball's trajectory, they can associate its vertex with the ball's maximum height (484 feet) and thereby better understand the concept of a parabola. Even though the task involves a tennis ball being launched from the roof, that isn't what students are learning about. Instead, the ball simply serves as a convenient frame for illustrating an underlying mathematical concept. Students may be looking *with* something real from the world...but they're looking *at* quadratics.

How about a more visceral approach like a multimedia makeover? If a teacher uses modern technology to pose a mathematical question, and if the situation *appears* more authentic than that of a textbook word problem, does that change what students are looking at? Consider the following activity from Desmos. In it, students see a photograph of a basketball player taking a foul shot. The image has been edited to show multiple instances of the ball, and students sketch a parabola to determine whether the ball will go through the hoop. In this case, would you say that students are using the world to look at math, or are they using math to analyze the world?

"Will It Hit the Hoop?"

Whenever I share the foul shot activity with teachers and administrators, some say that it's fundamentally different than a word problem like the tennis ball task. "In the tennis ball task," they reason, "students are using the world to learn about parabolas. Here, they're using parabolas to learn about basketball."

I disagree. If the foul shot activity were "about basketball," then students would emerge with a deeper understanding of the game. Maybe they'd leave class having learned something new about whether it's better to shoot underhanded or over. Or maybe they'd be able to explain where a defender should stand to have the best chance of blocking a shot without getting beat off the dribble. But they don't. When students finish the activity, they haven't learned anything new about basketball. Instead, everything they've learned is about the *shape of the trajectory*. Students learn that the trajectory of a foul shot is parabolic. They learn that a parabola is symmetrical about its vertex. If students are provided with the equation of the trajectory, they can discuss how to use it to determine the ball's maximum height or its position when it reaches the rim. When teachers assign the foul shot task, students learn a lot about parabolas, but they learn almost nothing about basketball. The activity *involves* basketball, but it's *about* quadratics. As with the tennis ball task, students are looking with the world...but they're looking at the math.

Math educators have been using rote tasks, word problems, and other similar activities for years. That's good. Students need to develop procedural fluency, understand mathematical concepts, and be able to solve problems in various ways. And the types of tasks that teachers have traditionally used – rote practice, word problems, and multimedia makeovers – can certainly help them do this. However, it's not enough for students just to look at math. They also deserve opportunities to look with it. Unfortunately, mainstream math education has historically overlooked these experiences. As a community, we tell students that math is useful in real life. And yet by treating mathematics primarily as an object of observation — not a tool to use but a museum piece to admire — we've effectively created the equivalent of an astronomy class in which we say to students, "This year we're going to learn how a telescope works...but we're never going to look at the stars."

So what does it mean to "look with math"? What does it mean to use mathematics to analyze the world around us? When we turn the telescope around and train math on reality, what new insights do students gain and how much more dynamic does math class become?

Looking With Math

In the Citizen Math lesson *Out of Left Field*, students construct parabolas and quadratic functions to explore questions of fairness in Major League Baseball. Baseball is the only professional sport whose playing surface varies by stadium. In the National Football League, every field has the same dimensions. In the National Basketball Association, every court has the same dimensions. In the National Hockey League, every rink has the same dimensions. But in Major League Baseball, every field is different. Some ballparks have outfield walls that are closer and shorter, while others have ones that are farther and taller. This suggests that some stadiums are easier for home runs than are others. So how does this affect the game?

Students use data from the analytics website Statcast to explore this issue. Since most pro ballplayers bat right-handed, most home runs go over the left field wall. According to Statcast, the average left-field home run is struck 3 feet above home plate, reaches a maximum height of 81 feet, and travels a distance of 378 feet. Using this information, students derive a quadratic equation to model the trajectory of the average home run: $h(d) = -0.00223(d - 187.2)^2 + 81$, where $h(d)$ represents the height of the ball and d represents its distance from home plate. When students graph this equation, they can compare the resulting parabola to the left-field wall of every pro ballpark, and then determine which stadiums are the easiest and most difficult for home runs. (To avoid overcrowding, the diagram on next page only shows the walls for three teams' stadiums: from left to right, Yankees, Cardinals, and Cubs.)

Judging from the graph, the easiest stadium for left-field home runs belongs to the New York Yankees. The hardest belongs to the Chicago Cubs, while the St. Louis Cardinals' is somewhere in between. Of course, students can be more precise than this. Armed with the knowledge that the left-field wall in Yankee Stadium is 318 feet from home plate, for instance, students can use their equation to determine how high the average home run ball is when it reaches this distance: $h(318) = -0.00223(318 - 187.2)^2 + 81 = 43$ feet.

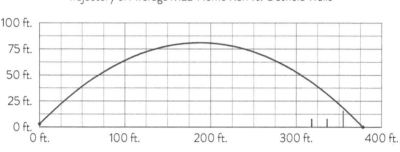

Trajectory of Average MLB Home Run vs. Outfield Walls

Since the Yankees' wall is 8 feet tall, the average home run would clear it by 35 feet. When students calculate the clearances in St. Louis and Chicago, they find that the average home run would clear their walls by only 24 feet and 3 feet, respectively.

How do these variations impact players? And should Major League Baseball require outfield dimensions to be standardized?

This is what students debate at the end of the activity. Some will argue that stadiums should be standardized, reasoning that it would make the game more fair and statistics more comparable. For instance, a baseball fan might cite the 1998 home run race between the Cardinals' Mark McGwire and the Cubs' Sammy Sosa. "Even though McGwire won," the student might reason, "he played half his games in an easier stadium. Because of differences in stadium construction, the contest wasn't legitimate." Another student might emphasize the impact that outfield dimensions have on player salaries. "If a pitcher is drafted by a team whose stadium left-field wall is low and close to home plate, he might earn less money over his career than he would have otherwise."

Other students will argue against standardization. A baseball purist might respond, "One of the best things about America's pastime is that pro stadiums are all different. Allowing teams to design stadiums differently preserves the charm that makes the game unique."

There's no right answer as to whether Major League Baseball should standardize outfield dimensions. When students debate this question, there's no expectation that they'll agree. What matters is that they consider opposing perspectives, justify their own reasoning, and ground their disagreements in mathematical analysis.

When students have opportunities to use math to explore authentic issues in the world, they're able to have conversations that haven't traditionally occurred in the math classroom: discussions that are informed by mathematics while being focused on the world. In the lesson *Out of Left Field*, students do a lot of math (some of it very difficult), and when they emerge, there's a good chance that they'll be better at manipulating equations and more familiar with how parabolas behave. But procedural fluency and conceptual understanding aren't the key takeaways of the activity. The goal is not for students to use home runs to understand parabolas. It's to apply parabolas to think critically about the relationship between home runs and outfield dimensions. The lesson involves a quadratic function...but it's about baseball. The next time students watch a baseball game, they'll see it in an entirely new way. That's what it means to "look with math." And if we want students to emerge from our classrooms with a complete math education, these are the kinds of experiences that we need to include in class.

Reality According to Math Class

As a community, we have historically neglected the role that math plays in helping us see the world more clearly. Instead of treating reality as something to be explored, we tend to value it only as a context for teaching mathematical standards. As I write this, the coronavirus is sweeping across the United States. Hundreds of thousands of Americans have died, with many more to come. Earlier this year, I saw a headline in the education section of the *New York Times* that revealed a lot about our priorities as teachers: "Teaching about Data and Statistics Using the Coronavirus Outbreak." Ponder that for a moment. *Using the virus to teach statistics.* It's totally backwards, yet we've become so habituated to using the world as a frame for looking at math that we don't even flinch. (It's as though God unleashed a pandemic just to throw stats teachers a bone.)

When we glorify *looking at math* but neglect *looking with math*, we dishonor the full nature of our discipline and rob students of a well-rounded learning experience. However, this one-way-only approach does more than alienate students from mathematics. It also alienates us from our students and undermines our credibility as teachers. To see why, consider the following word problem from Illustrative Math's Grade 8 curriculum.

Milkshake Task

Lin and Diego are drinking milkshakes. Diego starts with 20 ounces and drinks 2/3 ounce per second. Lin starts with 12 ounces and drinks 1/4 ounce per second. How long will it take Diego and Lin to finish their milkshakes?

At this point, I trust that you agree that this activity is not "about milkshakes" but that the authors simply used milkshakes as a way to set up a problem; in this case, one that requires modeling with linear functions. Students who are new to functions might answer the question by creating a table or drawing a glass divided into fractions. Other students might sketch a graph, while advanced students might write and solve equations: $20 - (2/3)s = 0$ and $12 - (1/4)s = 0$. There are plenty of ways for students to approach the activity. As an opportunity for students to experiment with different ways of solving a problem, the milkshake task is good.

But as an exploration of reality, the task is absurd. At the rates they're drinking, it'll take Diego 30 seconds to finish his milkshake and Lin 48 seconds to finish hers. Try drinking a milkshake for 48 seconds without stopping to breathe. Unless you're a whale or the winner of the Tour de France, it cannot be done. And yet that did not stop EdReports from giving the curriculum a perfect score, a score which they justified by explaining how "most units include a real-world application lesson" and help students "make connections to real-world contexts." The reviewers at EdReports specifically mentioned "real world" throughout their evaluation of the curriculum, even though there's nothing real about it.

The bending of reality isn't unique to Illustrative Math. If you open any textbook, you're likely to find many activities whose scenarios are unrealistic. Yet we rarely object. In fact, we barely notice. What this highlights is just how far down the rabbit hole we've gone as an educational community in viewing reality as a means to a pedagogical end. We tell students that mathematics is relevant in the real world, and yet the activities we assign operate within their own math-class version of reality: one in which kids can inhale ice-cream indefinitely thanks to lungs the size of Shamu's.

But students see through this. They know how traditional problems come about: a teacher or curriculum author is writing a unit on linear functions and thinks, "I need a context for linear equations. I've got it: milkshakes!" And because their goal is for students to look at math, they have no problem with manipulating the world or even distorting it beyond all recognition. It's no wonder, then, that students roll their eyes at math class, sigh, and ask, "Seriously, why are we learning this?" When milkshakes, magic purses, and gluten-rich chessboards are what we offer up as *real-world math*, we shouldn't be surprised when children conclude that mathematics is irrelevant. In fact, we should be shocked if they don't.

Reality According to Life

When our primary instructional goal is for students to solve linear equations, activities like the milkshake task are fine. But if we also want students to use linear equations to think critically about an actual issue in society, we don't have to contrive a reality. We just have to open our eyes to the real reality around us.

In towns and cities across the country, governments rely on sales and property taxes to maintain roads, builds schools, and fund other local services. In recent years, though, governments have increasingly turned to another source of revenue: fines. Speeding and parking tickets have become a central component in many regions' budgets. While fines have helped governments shore up their finances, they've had a dramatic impact on the lives of many residents, and low-income residents in particular.

To understand how municipal fines affect people differently, imagine two residents of the same city. Bo has a job that pays a monthly salary of $7,000. After taxes and expenses — a car payment, a nice apartment in a trendy neighborhood — Bo is able to save $200 each month. Meanwhile, Ali has a job that pays minimum wage. After paying for groceries, gas for her used car, and other frugal expenditures, Ali is able to save $50 every month.

While driving home from work one afternoon, Ali and Bo are both pulled over for speeding. If the ticket is $150, how many months' worth of savings will it take for each person to pay off the fine? In the Citizen Math lesson *You're So Fined*, students use linear equations to answer this, then discuss the implications.

Since Bo saves $200 each month, for him paying off the $150 ticket will require 0.75 months' (or three weeks') worth of savings. Since Ali saves less, it'll take her more: three months' worth. Is this discrepancy reasonable?

Some students will say that it is. "Bo and Ali committed the same violation, so they should face the same penalty." Other students will push back. "But the penalty isn't the same. Bo and Ali are paying the same number of dollars, but the ticket affects Ali more."

There are few issues that engage children more than questions of fairness, and this is a difficult one. Some students will argue something to the effect of, "If you can't pay the fine, don't do the crime," while others will muse about ways to base fines on the' ability to pay. In a classroom of thirty students, there's little chance that everyone will agree about the best approach, but that's okay. It's a valuable debate to have. For whatever students conclude about one-size-fits-all penalties, their disagreements will be rooted in mathematical analysis.

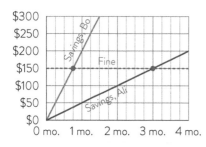

Months to Pay Fine, Bo and Ali

Bo	Ali
savings = fine	savings = fine
200m = 150	50m = 150
m = 0.75	m = 3
months = 0.75	months = 3

That said, this isn't where the speeding story ends. As you may know, in addition to the initial fine, many towns and cities in the United States add penalties for late payment. If Bo and Ali were charged $35 for every month that they couldn't pay off the fine, how long would it take and how much would the ticket end up costing? Students immediately reason that since Bo can afford to pay the $150 ticket in the first month, he won't be subject to the late fee. But Ali will. When students graph the new situation, they see that whereas the line representing the ticket was flat before, now it increases at a steady rate.

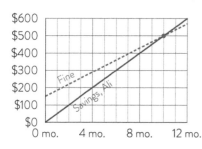

Months to Pay Fine and Fees, Ali

savings = fine
50m = 150 + 35m
15m = 150
m = 10

when months = 10,
fine = 150 + 35(10) = 500

When students calculate the new solution, they determine that Ali will now need 10 months to fully pay off her ticket, and she'll end up paying $500 in total: $150 for the initial fine plus $350 in late fees. Does this seem reasonable? If not, what should the city do instead?

When local governments began adding penalties for late payment, they did so because they saw it as a straightforward way to strengthen municipal budgets. Unfortunately, the policy comes with an unintended consequence. It leaves low-income residents in a vulnerable position and can trap them in a cycle of debt. If Ali has to spend every penny of her savings to pay down a speeding ticket for a full ten months, what happens if her car breaks down or her kid gets sick? I've facilitated this discussion with hundreds of students, teachers, and administrators. In many cases they were unaware of the impact that municipal fines were having on others in their communities. Yet even when everyone agrees that Ali's situation is unfair, they don't always agree on how the city should respond. It's a difficult issue.

It's also a real issue. In 2014, residents of Ferguson, Missouri, took to the streets to protest the police shooting of Michael Brown. While the shooting was the spark that lit the fuse, according to Attorney General Eric Holder, there was an additional reason that residents were so angry at law enforcement: the city's longstanding reliance on tickets and fees. "Local authorities consistently approached law enforcement not as a means for protecting public safety," Holder explained, "but as a way of generating revenue."

Of course, there's no getting around the fact that local governments need revenue to fund important services. Even after the protests in Ferguson died down, the financial realities remained. Towards the end of *You're So Fined*, students consider the issue from the government's perspective. In particular, they imagine that the city where Ali lives needs to raise more revenue, and they debate between two options: increasing the initial speeding fine or increasing the monthly late fee.

"If the city increased the initial ticket," a student may reason, "the line representing the fine would shift up. Now it would take even longer to intersect with Ali's savings line, and she'd end up paying more in total. This is a bad outcome."

Another student might disagree. "Raising the monthly fee could be worse. For instance, if the city increased the fee to $50 or more, the fine and savings lines would never intersect. Ali would spend her savings on fees forever but never pay off the ticket."

When students compare the city's proposals, they may describe the lines as "shifting up" or "getting steeper," or they might use more formal terms like "y-intercept" and "slope." To calculate how many months it will take to pay off the ticket, some students will draw graphs, while others prefer equations. But whatever language students use and whatever problem-solving strategies they employ, they're using them in the service of a larger discussion.

Unlike traditional activities like the milkshake task, the lesson *You're So Fined* didn't begin with a specific mathematical goal; it didn't begin with a curriculum author searching for a context that required solving equations. Instead, it began when the author saw a news story on television about municipal fines, researched how they worked, and only then discovered the math involved. ("I've got it: linear functions.") Because the lesson was written with a different goal and from a different direction than traditional tasks — using math to understand the world, rather than using the world as a frame for contextualizing math — it results in a very different learning experience. The conversation that students have certainly *involves* math. But it's *about* a real issue that affects real people.

The question that students wrestle with in this activity is the same one that communities across the country are weighing: how to collect revenue for local services in a way that's fair to residents. If we as a society hope to address issues like these constructively, we need to discuss them rationally...which means we need to analyze them algebraically. The math classroom is the ideal setting to learn how to do this, and math educators are the perfect people to show us how.

The Benefits of Looking with Math

For teachers accustomed primarily to the "looking at" side of math instruction, activities in which students explore social issues can feel unfamiliar, even scary. And because educators aren't required to prioritize real-world discussions — indeed, because the Common Core and other standards don't even require that the "real world" be real! — it can be easy to justify excluding them. However, there are three important benefits I've seen arise when teachers provide students with consistent opportunities to use mathematics to analyze the real reality around them.

The first benefit is that doing so demonstrates to students why mathematics is so useful and, more importantly, allows them to think critically about important and thought-provoking issues. A few years ago, a sixth-grade teacher in California forwarded my colleagues and me a note that one of her students had written. She had just finished teaching a lesson in which students use box-and-whisker plots to analyze wealth distribution in the United States, and a student handed her a Post-It Note with her reaction. "Amazing," the child had penned. "This really opened my eyes to the world we live in." When students use procedures and concepts to explore a topic like wealth inequality, they no longer need to ask when they'll ever use mathematics. That question will cease to occur to them.

The second benefit of having students use math to explore reality is that it makes being a teacher more fun. When I was in the classroom, I knew I had a responsibility to help students develop automaticity, but I still found skills practice dull. Even when it came to conceptual understanding, I found the activities uninspiring. As a math educator, I could appreciate the utility of questions like "How many pennies fit in a circle?" But as a human, I really didn't care.

Have you ever felt that tension between duty and passion? If so, you're not alone. A teacher in Kentucky once wrote a blog post about how burned out she felt from the tasks that have traditionally defined math instruction.

"I have spent most of the last three weeks feeling as though I am failing miserably," Brooke Powers shared honestly. "I spent the weekend with teacher burn out on my mind. Although I had already made a week's worth of plans and copies, I knew it was time to throw them out the window and find some lessons that would help reignite my passion for teaching."

She went on to describe the lessons she taught instead. In one, students calculated unit rates to compare how much teachers and pro athletes make per day, hour, and minute, then debated whether the job that pays the most is necessarily the one that's *worth* the most. In another, students used proportions to project how much time they'd spend over the course of their lives doing various activities, then discussed how this might influence their behavior. "We spend over one-third of our lives at work," Brooke explained at the end of her post. "That is why it is so important to find something you love to do. I was able to spend the first two days of this week falling in love with my classroom all over again."

Given how stressful school can be — dozens of standards to cover; end-of-year tests to prepare for — it can be easy to get distracted by roles like "teacher" and "student." When we allow math classrooms to become forums for meaningful conversations, we rekindle the common humanity that drew us to teaching in the first place.

The third benefit of using mathematics as a lens for thinking critically about the world may be the most critical of all: It erodes the certainty that increasingly undermines civil discourse in America. From Fox News to MSNBC to the videos recommended on Facebook, we are inundated with messages that reality is black and white and assurances that whatever we believe, we're absolutely right. This is dangerous. Very few answers to the questions we confront as a society are as self-evident as the media suggest. The more calcified our certainty becomes, the less sustainable our democracy will be.

And yet consider some of the real-world questions that we've explored thus far. *Should everyone in the country be required to buy health insurance? Should Major League Baseball standardize stadium dimensions? What's the fairest way for cities to raise revenue?* All of these questions are explorable in math class, but none has a right answer. Such questions have never been part of the mainstream math experience. From *How many meatballs fit in a pot?* to *Will the ball go through the hoop?*, the activities that math educators have historically prioritized all converge on a single answer. In fact, we're so accustomed to this that when we describe a math task as being "open-ended," what we usually mean is that there are multiple ways to get to a single answer.

Of course, closed-ended tasks have their advantages; it would be hard to teach addition, for instance, if 2 + 2 weren't always 4. However, an exclusive emphasis on them has an important downside. Many children associate being smart with being good at math. They also associate being good at math with getting the right answer. By the transitive property, then, math educators have unwittingly created a situation in which students conclude that being smart means getting the right answer...which of course presupposes there is a right answer to get. Not only is this all-or-nothing dichotomy intimidating to students who struggle with math, what's worse, it's exactly the fallacy that's undermining our ability to function as a democracy. From cable news to social media, we are constantly spoon-fed the message that if someone thinks differently about an issue in the world, it's because they're wrong (or dumb, racist, tyrannical, evil, etc.). If the only questions that students encounter in math class are ones with definitive solutions, then we as educators won't just miss an opportunity to erode the certainty that undermines constructive discourse. We might inadvertently exacerbate it.

For self-governance to succeed, citizens must be willing to acknowledge the possibility that when two people disagree, it could be because one of them is engaged in faulty thinking...but it could also be because the question they're debating doesn't have a definitive answer. When math educators create opportunities for students to analyze and discuss relevant issues in society, we help them understand the need to consider issues from multiple perspectives: that of insurance company and low-risk consumer; that of city mayor and low-wage resident. When it comes to the individual mandate, there's a decent chance that students from conservative backgrounds and those from liberal backgrounds will disagree. But consensus isn't the goal. The goal is for students to think logically about the issue, to consider one another's reasoning, and to ground their disagreements in math. By turning your classroom into a forum for discussing questions like "Should airlines overbook their flights?" and "Should fast food restaurants rewrite their menus in terms of exercise?" — questions that require math but do not have right answers — you help students resist the siren song of certainty and develop an appreciation of the legitimacy of informed ambivalence.

Honoring Math's Full Nature

Several years ago I participated in a workshop with a few dozen other math educators in Atlanta. The facilitator divided us into groups and instructed us to close our eyes and envision our ideal math class. After a minute or two, he asked us to open our eyes and share our responses with our tablemates.

A teacher to my left began. "I envision students working together on a problem," she said, "and comparing their various approaches for solving it."

"I envision students not giving up when they encounter a challenging question," another followed, "and being okay if they get the wrong answer."

"Too many people are frightened of math," an educator professor chimed in. "In my vision of an ideal classroom, I see every student discovering the joy of mathematical problem solving."

I raised my hand. "It seems like everyone envisions students becoming better problem solvers," I observed. "Does anyone have an opinion about the actual problems that they're solving?" I offered an example. "Imagine you're teaching a unit on solving linear functions. One task asks students to calculate how long it will take for someone to drink a milkshake. Another has them compare how long it will take for people with different incomes to pay off a speeding ticket. Do you see any difference between these two problems?"

"No," a teacher responded. "As long as students are solving equations and justifying their answers, I have no preference. The problems seem the same to me."

For generations students have asked why they're learning math and when they'll ever use it. Even when teachers incorporate new strategies (such as having students work in groups instead of alone) or adopt new ways of framing problems (such as with a video instead of wordy prose), millions of children continue to conclude that mathematics is irrelevant to real life. This is a clear indication, then, that the fault lies not just in how we teach but in what we teach. The fault lies with the problems themselves, and specifically with our historical failure to distinguish between math as something to look at and math as something to look with. The milkshake and speeding activities both have important roles to play in math class, but those roles are very different. To almost everyone on the planet, how long it takes to drink a milkshake and how long it takes someone earning minimum wage to pay off a municipal fine are not equivalent problems. They're not even close. And the only place they'd be treated as such is the math classroom.

If we're to offer students a complete experience of learning mathematics, then we must honor both aspects of its character. Once we do that — and once students are consistently using math to learn *about the world* and not just learning *about math* — we'll take a giant leap towards fulfilling our potential as stewards of an analytical society. And honestly, isn't that why you became an educator in the first place? When you close your eyes and imagine your ideal classroom, are you content talking only about procedures and concepts and teaching only the tasks that have long defined math class? Do you envision yourself also facilitating conversations that challenge students to turn the telescope of mathematics around, to train it on the actual world so that they can live more intentionally in it?

OVERSELLING FLIGHTS

Should airlines oversell their flights?

mathematics used: compound probabilities, combinations, and expected value

O N April 9, 2017, United Airlines made headlines when police officers at Chicago's O'Hare Airport were filmed dragging passenger David Dao from Flight 3411 as the plane sat parked at the gate waiting to depart. Cell phone videos quickly spread of Dao, his nose broken and face bloodied, begging not to be removed. "I have to go home," the 69-year-old doctor pleaded, explaining that he had patients back home in Kentucky that he needed to treat.

Why was Dao forced from the plane? Had be been acting erratically? Had he made a terrorist threat before the plane took off? No. United had simply oversold the flight. The airline sold more tickets than there were seats on the plane, and it needed to make room. At first, flight attendants offered vouchers to anyone who would voluntarily give up their seat. When nobody accepted, a computer randomly selected passengers to be removed, including David Dao. When he refused to give up his seat, the airline ordered him removed.

As someone who flies a lot, I must admit: this story made me mad. Yet as frustrating as this specific incident was (and as extreme as United's decision seemed), the underlying situation is not uncommon. Airlines regularly oversell their flights, and for good reason: ticketholders often don't show up at the gate. Depending on the route and time of year, anywhere from 5 to 15 percent of passengers might miss a given flight; maybe they got caught in traffic or maybe their connection was delayed. Whatever the reason, instead of potentially flying with empty seats, an airline might sell the same seat twice, pocketing the extra revenue...and hoping that not everyone shows up.

To better understand the rationale behind this strategy, let's consider a typical scenario: a flight on an airplane with 150 seats and a "no-show" rate of 10 percent. If the airline sold 150 tickets, then it would only expect 135 passengers to show up. Of course, it's possible that fewer would. It's also possible that more would. But 135 is the most likely number, which would mean a partially empty plane. If the airline sold 166 tickets, on the other hand, then the expected outcome would be a full flight with 150 passengers. (Mathematically, we'd expect 149.4 passengers to show up. But since fractional passengers aren't possible, we round up to the next whole number.) Meanwhile, nobody would be left angrily stranded at the gate, and the airline would get to keep 16 tickets' worth of free revenue. Still, just because an outcome is the most *likely* doesn't mean that it is likely. If the airline sells 166 tickets for a 150-seat flight with a 10 percent no-show rate, then, what is the probability that exactly 150 passengers show up? To answer this, we need to use two different mathematical topics: compound probabilities and combinations.

For the first part of our analysis, let's treat the flight like a coin toss, where showing up for the flight is "heads" and missing the flight is "tails." Since we'll flip the coin 166 times — once for each customer who bought a ticket — what we want to determine is the probability of flipping heads 150 times in a row followed by tails 16 times in a row. Unlike with a normal coin, though, our "flight coin" is weighted; it has a 10 percent chance of landing on tails (no show) and thus a 90 percent chance of landing on heads (show). Given this, we can use the following expression to find our desired probability:

Probability of 150 shows followed by 16 no-shows

$$(0.90)^{150} \cdot (0.10)^{16}$$

When we perform the calculation, we get a result of $1.37 \cdot 10^{-23}$. This is very close to zero. In other words, if you placed all 166 ticketholders in a line, it's extremely unlikely that the first 150 of them would be the ones who arrive to the flight on time and the last 16 would be the ones who don't.

Then again, this isn't actually what we're after. We're not interested in the specific order in which the coin lands. All we care about is that, in 166 flips, it lands on heads 150 times and on tails 16 times. While 150 heads *followed* by 16 tails is not a likely result, it's also just one of the many orderings that achieves our desired split. For the second part of our analysis, then, we need to determine the total number of ways there are for 166 flips to result in 150 heads and 16 tails (representing the total number of ways to organize a group of 166 ticketholders into 150 shows and 16 no-shows).

Total ways to arrange 166 customers into 150 shows and 16 no-shows

$$\frac{166 \cdot 165 \cdot 164 \cdot \ldots \cdot 1}{(150 \cdot 149 \cdot 148 \cdot \ldots \cdot 1) \cdot (16 \cdot 15 \cdot 14 \cdot \ldots \cdot 1)} = \frac{166!}{150! \cdot 16!}$$

As you might expect, this number is absolutely massive: $7.53 \cdot 10^{21}$. From a collection of 166 people, there are nearly 8 sextillion ways to arrange them into our desired show/no-show groups. That's a lot of possible orderings.

Now that we've performed our two calculations, we can determine the answer we're after. If the airline sells 166 tickets for a 150-seat flight, and if the flight has a no-show rate of 10 percent, then the probability that exactly 150 passengers show up can be found by multiplying the probability of any specific ordering times the total number of possible orderings.

Probably that exactly 150 of 166 ticketholders show up

$$(0.90)^{150} \cdot (0.10)^{16} \quad \cdot \quad \frac{166!}{150! \cdot 16!}$$

When we do this, we find that the probability is 0.1031, or just over 10%. Even though 150 passengers is the most likely outcome, it's still fairly unlikely. There are other possible outcomes, as well, ranging from nobody showing up to everyone showing up. If fewer than 150 ticketholders arrive at the gate, it won't be an issue; the plane will take off with a few empty seats. But if more than 150 ticketholders appear, someone will have to get bumped.

So what's the likelihood of this happening? The following bar chart shows the probabilities of different numbers of passengers showing up for the flight. For instance, the probability that exactly 151 of the 166 ticketholders arrive at the gate is a bit less than 10%; in this case, one person would have to give up their seat. The probability of exactly 152 people arriving is even lower: 9.8%.

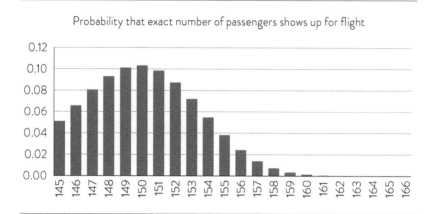

Probability that exact number of passengers shows up for flight

The greater the number of show-ups, the less likely the outcome becomes. Of course, there is some chance that all 166 ticketholders make the flight, but it's negligible: $2.53 \cdot 10^{-8}$, or roughly 1 in 40 million. When we add up all of the bars to the right of 150, we get a cumulative probability of 40%. In other words, even when the airline sells sixteen extra tickets for its 150-seat flight, it's still more likely than not that nobody will notice; that no passengers will have to get bumped.

But what if they do? If the 166 coin tosses land such that more than 150 people show up for the flight, what are the consequences for the airline?

In the United States, passengers who are involuntarily removed from a flight due to overbooking are legally entitled to compensation. Depending on the length of the delay, for a domestic flight the airline could be required to pay $1,300 to every passenger affected (in addition to rebooking them on the next flight). If 151 customers arrive for the 150-seat flight, the airline will only have to pay $1,300 in total compensation. But if all 166 customers show up, it'll be out nearly $21,000. Given this, why would an airline ever take the risk of selling more tickets than there are seats on the plane?

The reason, of course, has to do with the probability of each outcome. As we saw earlier, there's only a 9.8% chance that exactly 151 passengers show up at the gate. Even though the *actual* compensation from this outcome would be $1,300, the *expected* compensation is just $1,300 \cdot 0.098 = $127. Meanwhile, the expected payout from the worst-case scenario in which all 166 people show up is even less. Even though the actual payout would be substantial, because the outcome's probability is basically zero, then so is the downside that the airline projects.

Total Expected Payouts from Overselling

$$\sum_{p=150}^{166} (0.9)^p \cdot (0.1)^{166-p} \cdot \frac{166!}{p! \cdot (166-p)!} \cdot 1300(p-150)$$

When we add up what the airline would expect to pay in penalties from all sixteen overselling outcomes, we calculate a total expected payout of $1,618. That's nothing...especially when compared to the additional revenue that the airline earns by double-selling its sixteen tickets. If the airline charges an average of $350 per ticket, then it's effectively trading $5,600 in guaranteed upside for $1,618 in expected loss. To the actuaries who work at the company, this decision is a no-brainer. Thanks to the no-show rate, an airplane is effectively a casino with wings. Instead of asking whether airlines should oversell flights, perhaps a better question is why they don't oversell them by more.

In the wake of the 2017 controversy over United Airlines' treatment of David Dao, many airlines updated their overselling policies. Delta increased the compensation its agents could offer to incentivize customers to volunteer their seats. American promised that once passengers had boarded the plane, they would not be asked to move. Southwest did away with overbooking altogether. Yet while what happened in Chicago was clearly outrageous, the awfulness of the underlying issue is less clear cut. Air travel is an incredibly complex system. Every day there are more than 45,000 flights in and out of the United States. With weather delays, mechanical problems, and other inevitabilities, that means a lot of missed connections and thus a lot of empty seats. The more of these seats that airlines can fill, the fewer planes they'll need to send, the less carbon dioxide there will be in the atmosphere, and the less crowded airports will become. Not only that, but since overbooking means additional revenue for airlines, it might also mean lower ticket prices for travelers.

When a customer is forced to give up a seat that they paid for, it's easy to vilify airlines as being greedy and uncaring. As frustrating as this situation is for passengers, though, there's a logic behind overselling. Even if we don't like it, we should still understand it.

Discussion Questions

● In addition to the no-show rate, what are some factors that you think airlines should consider when deciding whether or not to oversell a particular flight?

● What are some changes that might reduce the no-show rate, and do you think these would be worth making? (For instance, if the FAA required pilots to wait for delayed passengers, would that be an improvement?)

● As a passenger, do you approve of airlines overselling flights?

PART FOUR

ADDRESSING COMMON CONCERNS

THERE'S a teacher in Indiana who demonstrates just how influential math educators can be in fostering an analytical and respectful citizenry. Alison Strole teaches at Fishers Junior High School in Fishers, Indiana, a town thirty minutes northeast of Indianapolis. I read about her in an article in *EdWeek* titled "Math: The Most Powerful Civics Class You've Never Had." The author explained how Mrs. Strole incorporated authentic real-world activities into her classroom, and then used them as jumping-off points for larger community engagement. As part of their systems of equations unit, students used linear functions to analyze the cost effectiveness of solar panels. When they finished, they learned that their city was building a new power plant, so they contacted the mayor to inquire whether the plan included renewable energy. The mayor responded by sending a representative from city hall to discuss energy policy with the class. As part of another unit on periodic functions, students used sinusoidal waves to compare the circadian rhythms of adults and teenagers. Upon discovering that their adolescent brains did not become fully alert until hours after school started, they petitioned the school board to consider delaying the start time and justified their reasoning with trigonometry.

As described in the article, Mrs. Strole's approach to math instruction represents a "missing piece in the national conversation about improving civics education: how math can be harnessed towards schools' goal of readying youths for engaged citizenship." Mrs. Strole still assigns activities on procedural fluency and conceptual understanding, of course. She hasn't dismissed traditional math instruction. She's added to it. By using mathematics as a lens for thinking critically about relevant issues and engaging respectfully with members of their town, Mrs. Strole and her students present a refreshing vision of what responsible citizenship looks like. In a few years these adolescents will graduate and assume the reins of the country. If America's future tomorrow resembles Mrs. Strole's classroom today, we may be in very good hands.

Alison Strole is an inspiring teacher, yet she isn't unique. Lots of us join the profession because we imagine ourselves as stewards of a math-minded citizenry. We recognize that mathematics is a powerful tool, and we aspire to help students use it to improve the world around them. Unfortunately, once we enter the classroom, many of us allow that image to fade. We still say that we want to make math real, but in practice we revert to the experience that's always defined math instruction: rote practice and word problems, math for math's sake. Why is this? If so many of us entered the classroom to do exactly what Mrs. Strole is doing, why do so few of us actually do it?

From what I've learned over the course of my career, there are a handful of reasons that educators commonly offer for not prioritizing authentic real-world discussions in math class. Each justification has merit and deserves an honest airing. At the same time, each is rooted in flawed assumptions and demands to be addressed.

Pushback 1: "I'm Already Making Math Real"

One reason that math educators often fail to incorporate authentic real-world activities into their classrooms is because they assume they already are. "During our linear functions unit," a teacher might explain, "we estimated how long it would take to drink a milkshake. During our quadratics unit, we determined whether a foul shot would go through a hoop. In my classroom, students use math to explore the world all the time."

It's wonderful when teachers and administrators want to make mathematics relevant for students. It's sad to say, but there are plenty of educators in the country who don't care whether kids find math useful or whether they can apply it to real life. In some cases it's because a teacher finds the subject so intriguing in and of itself that they see no need to apply it; they view mathematics solely as a puzzle to solve rather than also a tool to use. In other cases it's because a teacher has been stuck in the same do-this-then-do-that groove for so long that they're intractably resistant to change. "I've been using the textbook forever," such a teacher might say. "If it was good enough for the last class, it's good enough for the new class." When students ask when they'll ever use math, such an educator might dismiss the question, the classroom equivalent of "get off my lawn." However, when educators do attempt to integrate authentic activities into their instruction, they demonstrate respect for students' concerns and a commitment to a complete mathematics education.

Unfortunately, even when students are given opportunities to explore seemingly "real-world" situations like milkshakes and foul shots, many still conclude that mathematics has no bearing on real life. Again, the reason is that math educators don't always distinguish between using the world as a context for illustrating math and using math to explore the world. We math educators need to get better at distinguishing between what a task *involves* and what a task is *about*. There are two strategies that educators can use to do this. One strategy is to ask, when evaluating an activity, "What do I expect students to remember a week from now?" If the main takeaway is mathematical, the task is likely *about math*. If the takeaway is about the specific real-world situation at play, the activity is *about the world*.

For example, when evaluating the milkshake task, a teacher might think, "A week from now, I want students to remember how to write and solve an equation in the form $mx + b = 0$." However, the teacher would not expect kids to recall the sizes of Lin's and Diego's cups or even that they were drinking milkshakes in the first place. This task *involves* the world but is fundamentally *about* the math, and we should therefore avoid giving it credit for being an authentic real-world activity. Contrast this with the *You're So Fined* lesson about speeding tickets. Here, when a teacher considers the main takeaways, they're likely to say, "I want students to remember that municipal fines affect some people more than others. I also want them to keep thinking about the fairest ways for cities to generate revenue." Since the primary takeaway here is fundamentally social, the teacher can conclude that the activity is *about the world* and can designate it as an authentic real-world exploration.

The second strategy that educators can use to correctly determine whether an activity truly makes math real is to consider the centrality of the context. When evaluating a task, a teacher can ask, "If I replaced the current context with another, would that change students' experience?" If the context can be replaced without altering the underlying learning experience, it's *about* a mathematical process or concept and the task should not be designated as an authentic real-world activity. If the context cannot be replaced, the teacher can conclude the opposite.

Take the foul shot activity. Instead of having students predict whether a basketball will pass through a hoop, what if the task asked them to predict whether a rotten apple will land in a trash can? Would changing the context change students' underlying experience? Not at all. It doesn't matter what projectile is being thrown. All that matters is that students use a parabola to model its trajectory. Since basketball isn't strictly necessary, the task must not be about basketball at all. On the other hand, in the lesson *Out of Left Field*, replacing baseball with another context would undermine the student experience. In this lesson, students use a home run's trajectory to discuss whether outfield walls should be standardized. If the task were rewritten to swap the baseball for an apple, the conversation would lose all meaning. Since the specific context is central to the learning experience, the teacher can conclude that the activity is *about baseball* and deserves credit for being an authentic exploration of reality.

(This does not mean that students couldn't use similar mathematics to explore a different situation. Students could use parabolas to discuss when a football team should attempt a field goal or when a golfer should switch from an iron to a wedge. However, this wouldn't involve simply swapping baseball for another context. It would entail a completely different lesson with its own context-specific information. The math would be similar, but students' conversations and takeaways would depend on the sport.)

Thoughtful educators are trying to make mathematics relevant for their students, yet many children continue to conclude that the math they're learning in school is disconnected from real life. Many teachers find this baffling. "We did the milkshake and foul shot activities," they reason. "How can students say that math isn't useful?" The problem is not with the tasks themselves. The problem is with the misdiagnosis of the role that such tasks play in math instruction.

Pushback 2: "These Discussions Are for Other Teachers"

Another reason that math educators often resist incorporating real-world discussions into their classrooms is because they think that other teachers are better equipped to facilitate them. "My role is to teach the mathematics that students will need in the world," a teacher might reason. "It's another teacher's role to discuss how the world works." When math teachers say this, it isn't because they're uninterested in discussing relevant issues with their students. It's often because they assume they lack the necessary expertise to manage the discussions correctly.

At first glance, this seems reasonable. Take an issue like opioid addiction. Humans have been using opioids for centuries to treat pain. In recent years, however, opioids have become an epidemic. In 2019, more than 50,000 Americans died from overdosing on drugs such as OxyContin and heroin. If we as a country are to resolve this crisis, then we need students to understand what's behind it (and maybe even help to solve it). Since opioid addiction is a social issue that affects human health, it makes sense that the most appropriate educators to explore it would be the social studies teacher, the health teacher, and the school nurse. After all, they're the ones who seem to possess the relevant tools and backgrounds.

In fact, math educators have an important role to play in helping students understand the issue. When someone gets sick or injured, their doctor may prescribe an opioid to relieve their pain. The longer the human body is exposed to the medication – in other words, the longer the patient takes it – the less pain relief each individual dose provides. Doctors refer to this phenomenon as "opioid tolerance," and pharmacologists sometimes model it using exponential decay. For instance, when a patient first starts taking a pain medication, it might provide 10 out of 10 units of pain relief. After thirty weeks, however, it might only provide 5 units of relief, and after sixty weeks 2.5 units of relief. What this means is that if someone recovering from an injury or surgery wants to be pain-free, they may compensate by taking more doses over time.

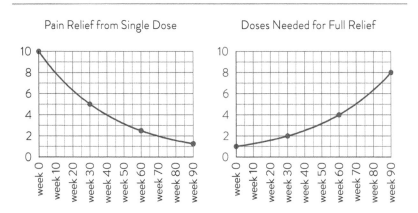

When patients take more pain medication than their doctors recommend, their decision is understandable; it's a logical response to a physiological phenomenon. But there are a number of unfortunate consequences. When someone's prescription runs out, they can suffer withdrawal symptoms such as nausea and restlessness. Many patients seek to avoid these by acquiring pills illegally, either by stealing them or buying them on the black market. Others turn to more potent opioids like fentanyl, a narcotic that's so powerful that just a few granules can prove fatal. Opioids work by suppressing many of the body's natural responses. This includes its response to pain...as well as its instinct to breathe. When people fatally overdose on opioids, it's often because they took so much of the drug that it caused their breathing to stop.

Opioid addiction is an important issue, and school offers a unique opportunity for children to learn about it. When math educators say that they're not the ones to facilitate discussions about topics like these, they mean well. They want students to have the best possible learning experience — one that honors not just the complexity of the issue but also those affected by it — and they assume that other teachers are the ones to provide it. They're not wrong. The health teacher absolutely has a role to play in helping students understand the biology of addiction. The social studies teacher is a great person to explore the history of government regulation and the tension between individual responsibility and social welfare. When it comes to whether doctors are violating their Hippocratic Oath by prescribing medications they know to be addictive, that's a perfect discussion for the school nurse to lead.

Still, just because other educators have a contribution to make doesn't mean that math teachers don't also. They do. Students cannot understand the addiction crisis without also understanding the exponential decay that underlies it, and the math teacher is the one to help them do this. If the math teacher works in a school that prioritizes collaborations between content areas, that's terrific; what powerful takeaways students would have if the math and social studies teacher planned a unit on opioids together! But even if educators operate in disciplinary silos (which is the case in most schools) — even if the social studies teacher and health teacher and school nurse never broach the topic of opioid addiction — the math teacher still can. And, I'd argue, must.

Again, I know how strange this may sound to educators accustomed to our traditional approach to math instruction. As a community, we are not accustomed to thinking about math class as place to discuss relevant social issues, nor are we used to thinking of ourselves as capable facilitators of real-world conversation. And yet consider the issues. *Should school start later in the morning to accommodate adolescents' sleep cycles?* This seems like an obvious discussion for health class, but it requires sinusoidal functions. *How much plastic do we waste when we buy disposable water bottles?* This seems like a question for science class, yet it involves the surface area of a cylinder. *What's the highest building floor that a ladder can safely reach?* This is clearly a discussion for shop class, right? How could it be otherwise? Because determining the maximum ladder height requires the Pythagorean Theorem...and teaching that is not the job of the shop teacher.

When math educators seek to outsource real-world conversations to other classrooms, it's usually because they maintain an overly narrow conception of what mathematics is: a set of procedures, concepts, and problem-solving strategies. But as you now know, math is also a lens to look at the world around us, and math class can serve as a survey course across reality, an opportunity to discuss everything under the sun: from the proper way to adjust a car's mirrors (angle bisectors) to whether college is worth the cost (linear functions); from accuracy in government surveillance (compound probabilities) to racial bias in death penalty sentencing (two-way tables). There are very few issues in the world that cannot be better understood using math, which means there are very few educators with as diverse an intellectual playground as math teachers.

Still, it can be intimidating to facilitate discussions about social questions, especially ones that lack definitive answers. Math teachers want what's best for their students, and it can be hard to overcome the nagging feeling that they lack the expertise needed to do a topic justice. But here's the thing: nobody has perfect expertise. A math teacher may not know everything there is to know about opioids, but neither does anyone else: not the health teacher, not the social studies teacher, not the school nurse. As educators, we should be aware of our limitations, but we should also remember what school exists to do. The purpose of school is to expose children to new ideas and to help them develop the tools they'll need to explore them.

School is the *beginning* of a learning process, not the end, and certainly not the totality. The math classroom is *not* where students will develop a comprehensive mastery of all things opioid; that place doesn't exist. Instead, it's the setting where students can begin their intellectual journey, the room from which they emerge with a clearer understanding of the world around them: not a perfect understanding, but a better one.

If you're a math educator, you may be asking yourself, "Who am I to lead a conversation about opioid addiction, baseball stadiums, and municipal fines? I'm comfortable with the math. But who am I to discuss the world?" The answer is simple: *You're a teacher. You're a leader in your community. You're the person society has asked to incubate a better version of itself.* Who are you to lead conversations about the world around us? You're exactly who we need.

Pushback 3: "The Topic is Too Sensitive/Controversial"

Even when math educators are willing to incorporate authenticity into their instruction, there may be some topics which they fear are too sensitive or controversial. A teacher might think, "I'm happy to use quadratics to analyze baseball stadiums, but opioids and health insurance are too fraught for school."

In my experience, educators typically have two concerns in mind. One is that students won't be able to discuss sensitive or controversial issues maturely. The other is that parents and community members will hear that students did a lesson on opioid addiction and call the school principal to complain. "I think it's important that students analyze the overdose crisis," a teacher might think, "and I know that exponential decay is a helpful tool for doing that. But the country has become so charged. The lesson isn't worth the headache."

When a math teacher presses pause on a prospective conversation because they're concerned that it'll open a Pandora's box, it demonstrates a remarkable level of thoughtfulness and integrity. These teachers respect how difficult certain discussions may be, and they opt to defer to the pedagogical version of the Hippocratic Oath: *first, do no harm.*

As reasonable as this deferral is, it has a very harmful consequence. As a country, we are bad at talking to one another about many issues, but especially those that one might characterize as "controversial." In a previous era, perhaps we could have relied on unbiased news anchors and responsible elected leaders to help us think objectively about the challenges we face. Today, though, much of the media profits by encouraging us not to think by calcifying certainty and rendering constructive discourse less likely. If America's democratic experiment is to succeed, math class must serve as a bulwark against irrational backsliding.

Fortunately, it is possible for math teachers to incorporate into their classrooms explorations of challenging real-world issues in a way that amplifies student maturity and minimizes the likelihood of disgruntled phone calls. Here are three approaches.

The first is to approach the real-world activity as a conversation to participate in rather than a lesson to lead. Math educators often believe it's their responsibility to know all of the answers about a given question and to guide an activity to a particular outcome. While this makes sense when it comes to a closed-ended topic like the solution to an equation, when applied to an issue like health insurance, it can stifle the discussion, put students in a position to tailor their responses to what they assume the teacher wants to hear, and make the exploration seem like a charade. When an educator enters the classroom with the mindset of, "I may be more familiar with the mathematics behind insurance markets, but when it comes to the individual mandate I'm just one voice and am interested in what students have to say," it removes much of the pressure and adds a much-needed feeling of authenticity into the classroom conversation.

Not too long ago I facilitated a lesson in which middle schoolers used linear regressions to compare income, rent, and homelessness in three American cities: New York, Los Angeles, and Seattle. I asked which city they thought had experienced the highest overall rise in living costs, expecting that students would compare income and rent in dollars. However, when one student decided to compare rents as a fraction of income, I was taken aback. "Huh," I said. "I hadn't thought of that." Had I approached the activity with the belief that my role as a teacher was to be the all-knowing *sage on the stage*, I would have felt flustered, maybe even intimidated. Because I saw myself simply as one human among dozens, I was able to react the way that I would have at, say, a dinner with friends: "That's an interesting approach. Please elaborate."

It's a curious phenomenon. In our daily lives, participating in a free-flowing discussion is the most natural thing in the world. And yet as soon as we walk into a classroom, we often lose that sense of ease. It's important to regain it. For when we give ourselves permission to not have all the answers and to treat students as conversational equals, we communicate a powerful message: *We're in this classroom to discuss a real issue, and everyone's input is needed.* Not only does this recalibrate the power hierarchy that has historically characterized school, but also it puts the onus on students to live up to the expectation of maturity. In my experience, students tend to misbehave or act disrespectfully when they feel intellectually patronized. Once students internalize their teachers and peers as intellectual collaborators and math class as a forum for conversations about authentic issues, they're much more likely to approach discussions about sensitive and controversial topics with thoughtfulness and respect. And this begins, of course, with the teacher approaching the activity thinking, "My role is to facilitate a discussion in which we use mathematics to discuss health insurance, and I'm eager to hear what students think."

The second approach that educators can use to successfully incorporate activities about difficult topics is to avoid treating them as contexts for teaching math. If we want children to take an issue seriously, then we have a responsibility to take it seriously, too. When we use the world merely as a setup for exploring a mathematical process or concept, we undermine a situation's gravity and unwittingly invite students to do the same. A friend once shared with me a word problem he'd written. The task involved a Syrian refugee who had been displaced from her home by a civil war. Each morning, the task explained, the child collected water by walking along the legs of a right triangle. The task asked students to calculate the distance the girl would save by walking along the hypotenuse instead.

By using such a serious situation for such a transparently mathematical purpose — a civil war a context for solving the Pythagorean Theorem — the task trivialized an important issue and implicitly allowed students to approach the conversation with less earnestness than it deserved.

When teachers differentiate between activities that use the world to contextualize math and those that use math to explore the world, they can better ensure that students approach conversations about challenging issues with maturity and seriousness. If during the lesson on opioids a student made a joke about patients taking too much medication, the teacher would be well-positioned to respond, "This is the reality that many Americans are facing. If you'd like to participate in this activity with us, we expect you to take it seriously." Educators often assume that children won't be able to handle discussions about sensitive and controversial issues. However, the solution to this isn't to avoid the activities. It's to be clear on what they're about before teaching them.

The final approach that teachers can use to successfully integrate authentic activities about difficult topics may be the most challenging: avoiding personal bias. Mathematics is a powerful tool for analyzing the world objectively. Still, none of us is a robot; we all have emotions and opinions. No matter how mightily we may try to facilitate a dispassionate discussion, it can be easy to tip our hand and reveal our personal bias.

During the opioids lesson, for instance, one teacher might think, "The federal government should crack down on pharmaceutical companies," while another might reason, "It's the patient's responsibility to make sure they don't take too much medication." If teachers aren't careful about checking their ideologies at the door, they might unintentionally steer the conversation towards a particular conclusion. While this danger exists in any class, it's especially pronounced in math. As highlighted by the famous quip, "lies, damned lies, and statistics," mathematics is frequently used to nefarious and dishonest ends. Because math is so powerful, we as educators must wield it cautiously and honor students' conclusions even if we disagree with them. In the *EdWeek* article about Alison Strole, the Indiana teacher perfectly articulates the importance of an unbiased approach to math instruction:

"I don't think it's my job to tell them how to think or feel. We live in a bubble on social media with people with like-minded opinions. I want [my students] to open it up and see both sides to arguments, and be able to support theirs with more than an opinion. And in my classroom, the support is the math."

When teachers avoid personal bias, they do more than create an atmosphere for students to discuss real-world issues freely and maturely. They also minimize the likelihood that someone outside of school will misconstrue the experience as indoctrination. Given how politically charged America is today, it's understandable when an educator thinks, "I'd love for students to use exponential functions to learn about opioids, but it seems risky. Maybe it's best if we just stick to magic purses." Fortunately, community pushback is less common than teachers might fear. I can only recall one instance in which a community member complained that a math class was discussing a sensitive issue...and even then the episode only ended up revealing how grateful people are for the unbiased and critical analysis that mathematics allows.

In 2017 a police officer in California happened upon the (then) Mathalicious website and saw that we had a lesson about excessive use of force. In the wake of years of news stories about fatal police shootings, the officer assumed that we were using the issue as a setup for math. Outraged, he called the local school district and asked them to stop using our lessons.

A few weeks later the officer and I spoke by phone.

"It's hard enough to convince the community that police officers aren't all bad," he explained. "The last thing we need is for teachers to make it worse."

I asked whether he had read the lesson in the time since he'd contacted the school district. He had not. So I walked him through what students actually do.

"Students analyze five years' worth of data from the Los Angeles Police Department to determine how excessive use of force complaints were distributed among its officers," I said. "They then use this distribution to evaluate the effectiveness of various potential strategies to reduce excessive force, from department-wide training to removing chronic offenders."

"Oh," the officer responded. "That sounds like a valuable thing for students to do. I wish we had done that when I was a kid."

No matter how badly a high-school teacher may want to help students think critically about authentic issues in the world, the prospect of having a parent or community member call the school can be terrifying. In my experience, though, people outside of education aren't concerned that schools are trying to help students think critically. They're concerned that teachers are pushing a political agenda. As divided as Americans are, one of the few things we agree on is the need to improve the substance and tenor of our discourse. When we as math educators make it clear that the only agenda we're pushing is that of quantitative examination, people don't just stop worrying. They become grateful.

Pushback 4: "My Students Aren't Ready"

How do viruses spread through a population? What's the best strategy for bidding on eBay? How much of what you see outdoors is an advertisement, and should cities get rid of billboards? Life is a cosmos of fascinating questions, and the math classroom is where we can discuss them. As interesting as these discussions are, though — and as much as some teachers say they'd like to facilitate them — educators often end up incorporating far fewer into their instruction than they might like. Their explanation? "My students aren't ready yet." Teachers reason that before students can apply mathematics to important and interesting issues, they must first master its procedures and concepts. "I'd like for students to analyze viruses and auctions," a teacher might think. "But first they must become fluent with exponential growth and polynomial functions."

The idea that students must *master* mathematics before they can *use* mathematics seems reasonable on its face. We often assume this about tools. Before astronomers can observe the stars, they must know how a telescope works. Before carpenters can build houses, they must become proficient with table saws. By the same reasoning, before students can discuss baseball stadiums and opioid addiction, they must learn everything there is to know about quadratics and exponential functions. Many educators think it's prudent to prioritize procedures and concepts before authentic applications; they want their students to be successful in their classrooms, and they assume this is the necessary order of operations. Not only that, but *learning math* before *using math* is what we are accustomed to. Textbooks and other materials have long used so-called "real-world" tasks as culminating activities: something for students to work towards, but not a step along the way.

As familiar as the mastery-before-application approach is, though, it has downsides. When students are only allowed to look with math once they've exhaustively looked at it, many conclude that mathematics is inaccessibly abstract and fail to develop a solid understanding of it. Predictably, these students perform poorly on quizzes and tests, prompting many educators to go back and re-teach the same material, leaving little time for the applied activities that they originally planned to end on...and causing students to question the value of learning math. And though educators assure them it's because they're going to "use it one day," the way they've organized their instruction ensures that *using math* is the one experience that students never get to have. After years of this, children reasonably conclude that mathematics is irrelevant, after all, and lose whatever motivation they may have had to learn it. This causes students to disengage even more, to perform even worse, and for many educators to double down even harder on the familiar approach to teaching. This downward spiral has plagued math education for centuries. Indeed, it's existed for so long that many educators don't even realize it's happening.

When educators suggest that students must master mathematical procedures, concepts, and problem-solving strategies before applying them to the world, there are two flaws in their reasoning. The first is that they fail to distinguish between informal knowledge and formal knowledge and the role that informal experiences can play in creating a solid foundation for subsequent mastery. The second flaw is that educators downplay the motivational impact of authenticity and how using math to explore real issues can give students a reason to learn it. By holding off on applying a mathematical tool until after students have mastered it, these educators overlook both how humans learn and why. When toddlers are learning to speak, they start by talking with family members, not by studying verb tenses or identifying "mama" as a noun. When humans develop a new skill, we typically begin intuitively and formalize later. Math educators, however, have inverted this process. By requiring students to master skills and concepts before using them, they effectively lead with the mathematical equivalent of grammar rules. This robs students of an opportunity to make sense of math and ensures that learning math is more difficult than it needs to be.

For instance, consider the way that many seventh grade teachers approach the skill of subtracting negative integers.

Positive Minus Negative	Negative Minus Negative
1,945 – (-40,000)	-40,000 – (-300,000)

When introducing students to this topic, teachers might begin by explaining the steps involved. "When subtracting a negative number," they might instruct, "the first thing do you do is change the minus sign to a plus. Next, if the numbers have the same sign, find the sum of their absolute values and keep the original sign. If the numbers have different signs, take their absolute values, subtract the smaller value from the larger value, and keep the sign of the larger original number." Based on these instructions:

$$1,945 - (-40,000)$$
$$1,945 + 40,000$$
$$41,945$$

$$-40,000 - (-300,000)$$
$$-40,000 + 300,000$$
$$300,000 - 40,000$$
$$260,000$$

The purpose of this exercise is to impart formal knowledge of integer subtraction. The teacher wants students to master the formal procedures involved in subtracting negative numbers and understand the formal concepts of absolute value and what it means for a quantity to be negative. The wording of the associated learning standard even sounds formal: *understand subtraction of rational numbers as adding the additive inverse, p − q = p + (-q)*.

If students are to emerge from math class with a rigorous understanding of mathematics, formal knowledge is a must. It's good that educators prioritize it. The problem is that they often prioritize it too early. To experienced educators, the steps involved in subtracting negative integers are clear and sensible. To children, though, they're devoid of meaning and can cause their eyes to glaze over. (Yours may have glazed over, too.) Even if students can initially follow the process for subtracting negative numbers, they're likely to forget it as soon as the teacher or textbook moves on to the next topic. Subtracting negative integers is a seventh-grade standard. Yet how many eighth-grade teachers have to re-teach it? How often do high-school teachers remediate middle school content, and how many art classes have been cancelled in order to double-block math? It's appropriate that teachers want students to appreciate the finer points of math. But when educators emphasize them prematurely, they become like grains of sand that slip through students' fingers.

Now consider an alternative approach. Instead of postponing authentic activities until after students have developed formal knowledge, what if educators used them as informal opportunities for students to discuss something real while also laying the groundwork for formal mastery? In the Citizen Math lesson *About Time*, students create a timeline showing the most significant inventions in three areas of human endeavor: communication, transportation, and warfare. In warfare, these innovations include the spear (300,000 BC), the bow and arrow (40,000 BC), and the atomic bomb (1945). How many years did it take humans to advance from one innovation to the next...and what might be some consequences of the length of successive jumps?

Milestones in Warfare

300,000 BC   40,000 BC   1945

To determine the time between each innovative leap, students may come up with various strategies. "To find how many years it took to advance from the spear to the bow and arrow," a student might reason, "I can go from 300,000 BC to 100,000 BC, which is 200,000 years. I can then go from 100,000 BC to 40,000 BC, which is another 60,000 years...for a total of 260,000 years." Another student might take a different approach. "To go from the spear to the bow and arrow, I can go from 300,000 BC to 0 AD, which is 300,000 years. I can then go backwards by 40,000 years, leaving 260,000 years." To quantify the leap between the bow and arrow and the atomic bomb, most students will do it in two stages: from 40,000 BC to 0 AD, then from 0 AD to 1,945, for a total of 41,945 years. (In reality, the Gregorian calendar does not include year 0 but progresses directly from 1 BC to 1 AD. By including it, though, we can simplify our calculations with little effect on the overall result.)

Whatever methods students use to find the lengths of the leaps, they're sure to find the results shocking. It took humans 260,000 years to advance from throwing a spear to shooting an arrow, but less than 42,000 years to advance from shooting an arrow to being able to incinerate the entire planet! This realization sparks a fascinating classroom discussion: *Are humans innovating faster than we can keep up with the consequences?*

As interesting as this conversation is, the mathematical process it involves is entirely accessible, even to students who hadn't previously encountered it. When students analyze the acceleration of warfare technology, the operations they're performing are the same as with the naked numbers approach: $1,945 - (-40,000)$ and $-40,000 - (-300,000)$. But since students are performing these operations in the context of an exploration of innovation, they may not identify the math they're doing as *subtracting negative integers*. In fact, if a teacher immediately followed the activity with a worksheet of practice questions, students might not be able to answer them. The knowledge hasn't been formalized yet. But the groundwork has been laid. Once students have contextualized subtraction as finding a distance along a timeline and strategized about using zero as a stopping point between negative and positive numbers, teachers will have a much easier time solidifying these intuitions into formal knowledge than they would otherwise. This is one of the benefits of using math before mastering it: the informal experience becomes a foundation to build on. To be sure, there are some skills and concepts that cannot be established informally, at least not on a school schedule. It might take weeks of toying with triangles for students to discover the Pythagorean Theorem, and it's unlikely that they'd ever derive the formula for the volume of a pyramid or the chain rule in calculus. In my experience, though, such instances are few and far between. In most cases the mathematical concepts and processes that students learn in school can be applied before being mastered, and often with better long-term results.

Take another topic that students historically struggle with: solving linear equations. When teachers introduce a problem such as solve for the value of x in $50x = 35x + 150$, they might instruct students to "subtract $35x$ from both sides, then divide both sides by 15." As a math educator, you probably appreciate the rationale behind these steps, but students may find them meaningless. On the other hand, students have no trouble determining how long it will take Ali, saving $50 each month, to pay off a $150 speeding ticket with a $35 monthly penalty. "After paying the penalty," a child may reason, "Ali has $15 left over at the end of each month. At this rate, it'll take her 10 months to pay off the $150 ticket." Students may not refer to 35 as the "slope" of the line or 150 as its "y-intercept," but that's okay. These are definitions that teachers can formalize later, building on the informal intuition that students have already developed.

That said, an activity doesn't have to be authentic to provide a stable foundation for mastery. It isn't strictly necessary that students explore real real-world issues like technological innovation or speeding fines. When it comes to subtracting negative numbers and solving linear equations, educators and curriculum developers have long invented scenarios to foster an intuitive understanding of math. Consider the two recent examples from EngageNY and Illustrative Math on the next page.

Mathematically, the airplane and plant activities do a fine job at helping students intuit an understanding of integer subtraction and equation solving.

Subtracting Negative Integers (EngageNY)	Solving Linear Equations (Illustrative Math)
An airplane flies at an altitude of 25,000 feet. A submarine dives to a depth of 600 feet below sea level. What is the difference in their elevations?	*Plant A starts at 6 ft tall and grows at a constant rate of 0.25 feet each day. Plant B starts at 3 ft tall and grows at a constant rate of 0.5 feet each day. After how many days will the plants be the same height?*

Even if students haven't yet been exposed to problems like $25,000 - (-600)$ and $0.25x + 6 = 0.5x + 3$, the contexts are such that children could probably figure out the answers. But would they *want* to? If kids encountered these questions outside of school, would they feel motivated to answer them? I doubt it. I imagine that most students would ask the same question that most non-students would ask: *Who cares?*

This brings up the second downside of the *look-at-math-first* approach. Even if contrived conceptual story problems are less confusing to students than their procedural counterparts, they can still sap students' motivation to learn, starting a downward spiral. A teacher launches a unit with a contrived "real-world" activity because they assume it'll be more mathematically accessible to students than an authentic real-world one. Students recognize the activity as contrived, reaffirm their suspicion that math is irrelevant, disengage from the learning process, and perform poorly on their assessments. The teacher then returns to square one to try again, eliminating any opportunity for students to use math to explore a real issue. Because the teacher assumed that students weren't ready to analyze the world, they never got a chance to try. It's the self-fulfilling prophecy that's haunted math classrooms for ages.

The mastery-first approach to math instruction that educators have long embraced overlooks a basic fact about human nature: When given a choice, we tend to learn something best when we care about it. In order for students to be willing to make the effort to master mathematics, they must first have a reason. Of course, students may have various reasons for wanting to succeed in math. These include extrinsic motivators such as a social need to appear smart in front of peers and an economic need to land a high-paying job. But according to some experts, the most powerful motivator is intellectual need, the intrinsic desire to learn in order to solve a compelling problem or answer an interesting question. When educators postpone real-world activities because they assume their students "aren't ready," they implicitly ask children to endure months of discussions about topics they find boring in order to (maybe one day) explore issues that they'll find interesting. It's as though American math education has staked its success on students being willing to indefinitely suppress their intellectual gag reflex. When educators say that students "aren't ready" to discuss the world, it isn't the children who aren't ready. It's the adults. *Mastery-before-application* is a mantra that educators have recited for so long that it's become gospel.

But it hasn't worked. On the contrary, it's responsible for many of the challenges that confront American math education. It's made learning math too hard, teaching math too frustrating, and math class way less cool than it could be. Fortunately, educators have an alternative: *not postponing real-world activities*. When students are given opportunities to apply math to real issues that affect real people, they quickly recognize the value of math and become more motivated to learn it. This isn't rocket science. It's human nature.

Children have been asking for years when they'll ever "use math." This is an excellent question. And it's a question that math educators are perfectly positioned to answer. From opioid addiction to wealth inequality, the acceleration of technology to police use of force, the world is full of interesting and important issues, and mathematics can help us explore them. When teachers prioritize using math to explore authentic issues early in students' learning process, they short-circuit the downward spiral of disengagement. Not only that, but they help students master mathematics more deeply than they would under the traditional mastery-first approach. Math educators have long treated reality as something to build towards. In fact, reality can be the platform for learning to launch *from*, the jumping-off point where mastery begins.

Pushback 5: It Won't Be on the Test

Of all the justifications that teachers offer for excluding conversations about real issues, the most common is the most straightforward: *It won't be on the test.*

A few years ago I visited an algebra classroom in New York. The teacher was doing a Citizen Math lesson in which students develop a quadratic function to model the relationship between the number of users on a social network and the number of possible connections between them. (If a network has two users, there's one possible connection. Three users: three connections. Four users: six connections. And so on.) Once students determine the equation,

$C = 0.5u^2 - 0.5u$, they apply it to Facebook to analyze how the number of possible connections has changed since the company was founded. Students conclude the activity by discussing whether social media platforms do connect users or whether, contrary to the mathematical model, they actually drive us apart. At least, that's how the lesson is supposed to end. In the classroom in New York, as soon as students wrote their equations, the teacher stopped the activity. "I'd love for them to discuss the societal effects of Facebook," she sighed to me afterwards. "But I don't have time. The state exam only asks students to write and evaluate equations. That's all they're required to know."

Every year millions of American students are required by law to take an end-of-year state assessment in math. In 2001, the federal government passed the No Child Left Behind Act, which mandated annual testing in grades 3-8 and once again in high school. If students performed well, teachers could receive bonus pay, depending on the area. If students performed poorly, the school could lose its accreditation and administrators could lose their jobs. In 2015 Congress replaced the law with the new Every Student Succeeds Act (ESSA), which allowed states to weigh additional factors such as attendance and access to advanced-placement courses. But end-of-year testing remained, and end-of-year scores continue to be the primary measure that administrators, parents, and others use when evaluating a school and the key outcome that teachers are held accountable to. As a result, many educators feel tremendous pressure to prioritize only those learning experiences that directly support the procedural fluencies and conceptual understandings the assessments measure.

For observers outside of education — parents, policymakers, editorialists — it's easy to criticize teachers for "teaching to the test." But that's unfair. They're just responding to the incentives that characterize American schooling. (Don't hate the player. Hate the game.) Still, deprioritizing real-life discussions saps the vitality from learning and alienates people from school. When children view classrooms as test-prep assembly lines, many disengage from their learning — and so do teachers. Every year thousands of math teachers leave the profession, and the number one reason they cite is the pressure of assessments and accountability. Given the vitality of childhood, you would think that a building full of children would be bursting with energy. Yet when you walk through the hallways of a school in America today, you're often struck by a profound sense of soullessness, a feeling of emptiness that leaves you exhausted and demoralized. The problem isn't the tests themselves. Tests (and the standardization of learning objectives more broadly) are useful. They provide teachers with concrete goals to work towards. They incentivize administrators to focus on all students, including English learners and special education students who may have been overlooked in a non-testing era. They make it easier for publishers of core curriculums to determine the efficacy of their materials and for organizations like EdReports to compare them on an apples-to-apples basis. Standardized tests play a helpful role in American education. The problem is that we've forgotten how limited this role was supposed to be. Year-end tests are designed to measure the bare minimum of what students are supposed to learn in a given year. The tests are a floor. Over time, however, we've turned them into a ceiling. Instead of using standardized assessments to inform some of what they do, many educators now allow the tests to dictate *everything* they do. As long as the end-of-year exams only ask students to look at math but not also to reason with math, that's all some teachers will make time for.

The reason this extreme focus on standardized testing is so problematic is because the tests are inherently limited. Authors of year-end tests can only include what they can reliably score, but what they can score is fairly low-level. In New York, the year-end Algebra 1 exam consists of 37 questions. Of these, 65% are multiple choice, 35% are free response...and 100% have closed-ended answers. On the 2020 test, for instance, questions on quadratics included:

NY Regents, Algebra 1, question 6

Which expression is equivalent to $18x^2 - 50$?

(a) $2(3x + 5)^2$
(b) $2(3x - 5)^2$
(c) $2(3x - 5)(3x + 5)$
(d) $2(3x - 25)(3x + 25)$

NY Regents, Algebra 1, question 32

Michael threw a ball into the air from the top of a building. The height of the ball, in feet, is modeled by the equation $h = -16t^2 + 64t + 60$, where t is the elapsed time in seconds. Determine the average rate of change, in feet per second, from when Michael released the ball to when the ball reached its maximum height.

For test administrators, questions like these are great. If students entered (c) and *32 feet per second*, they're right. If not, they're wrong. Students may have different ways of finding the right answer, but there's only one answer to find. Such items are easy to score. It would be very difficult, on the other hand, for officials to reliably evaluate a student's reasoning about whether Facebook is connecting or dividing America and whether baseball stadiums should be standardized. Even if evaluators could create a rubric to score these responses, it wouldn't matter. When it comes to state exams, the issue isn't whether a response can be scored. It's whether *millions* can be scored *quickly*.

This is not an argument for making standardized tests broader. It's an argument for not limiting education to them. When teachers opt not to explore relevant issues with students because they "won't be on the test," they restrict what students can learn — and what they themselves can teach — to what can be graded by a computer or easily categorized on a scoring key. As humans, the experiences we value most tend to lend themselves least to being quantified. It's easy to measure how many points a basketball player scored, but it's hard to measure her overall contribution to the team. If coaches can't quantify leadership, should they therefore deprioritize it? Similarly, it's trivial to determine whether a student can correctly write an exponential decay function, but it's impossible to quantify how deeply they empathize with someone suffering from opioid addiction. Should math teachers downgrade these conversations just because they're hard to measure? I don't think so. Abraham Lincoln described education as the "most important subject which we as a people can be engaged in." I can't imagine he was referring strictly to information that can be filled in a blank.

That said, you know this already. If you're still reading this letter after so many pages, you're probably an educator who desperately wants to go beyond the test but isn't sure how to do that in an environment so focused on testing. "I *do* want students to emerge from my class not just better at math but also more curious and thoughtful about the world," you may be thinking. "But responsible citizenship isn't on the test. How can I justify prioritizing it?"

As it turns out, using math to explore authentic real-world issues can in fact have a positive impact on standardized test results. In 2018, researchers from Northwestern University published the results of a 27,000-student study on the impact of authentic activities on year-end state test scores. The study found that teachers who incorporated just two real-world lessons into their curriculum saw test score gains that were equivalent to moving from average to the 80th percentile. What this suggests is that even when teachers use lessons that weren't specifically designed with standardized tests in mind, they can still help students develop the procedural fluencies and conceptual understandings that such tests assess.

Still, even if authentic examinations of the world didn't have an impact on standardized tests scores, they'd still be worth prioritizing. When teachers create space for themselves — or even better, when administrators create space for teachers — to prioritize mathematical conversations about thought-provoking issues, it helps keep their batteries charged. I've lost count of how many teachers (and coaches, principals, curriculum coordinators, assistant superintendents, etc.) have confided to me, "I don't know why I still do this." It isn't that they want standardized testing to go away, they say. They just don't want to lose all of their autonomy to it. They got into teaching to do something timeless...only to be told to prioritize an exam that could change in an instant and which no one will ever remember.

As educators, we have a responsibility to teach the skills and concepts that appear on the test, yes. But we also have a duty to honor why we became teachers in the first place: to inspire, and in a way that can't be measured.

Deciding To

Math class is much bigger than we've historically given it credit for, and math teachers can spark experiences that ripple far beyond the classroom. Remember the teacher featured in the *EdWeek* article, Alison Strole, and her students in Indiana. Using linear functions to analyze solar panels, then meeting with the mayor's office to discuss clean energy policy. Petitioning the local school board to shift the middle and high school start times, and grounding their reasoning in sinusoidal functions. It's a vision of what public education can be.

But even more, it's a reminder of what we can be as a country. As a citizenry, we have a hard time addressing the challenges we face, and we're only getting worse. Fueled by partisan news and emotion-stoking social media, our arguments are often unmoored from evidence and devoid of logic, and our discourse is a far cry from civil. And yet Mrs. Strole and her students invert this completely. "I want [my students] to...see both sides to arguments, and be able to support theirs with more than an opinion," she explains. "And in my classroom, the support is the math." This is more than a comment about unbiased teaching. It's a perfect distillation of responsible citizenship.

And yet Mrs. Strole's students aren't supernaturally gifted. Their school looks like any other school in America. Mrs. Strole faces the same challenges that other teachers do and could offer the same justifications that many others offer for not making math class real. Yet in spite of all of this, Mrs. Strole has transformed her classroom into a forum for authentic experiences and insights that her students will carry for the rest of their lives. Why is she able to accomplish what so many other teachers only daydream about?

Because she decided to.

RATING OUR EMOTIONS

What does an ideal week look like?

mathematics used: subtracting positive and negative integers; absolute value

A FRIEND of mine has an iPhone app that, once a day, asks him to rate how he's feeling on a scale from "couldn't be worse" to "really great." Mood tracking apps organize this data into charts and graphs which people can use to gain insights into themselves: when in the day they feel the highest; which types of activities leave them feeling the lowest. Yet as mood tracking becomes more ubiquitous, it's worth pondering: what is it that we're hoping to see?

Imagine four people rate how they're feeling at the end of the day. The charts on the next page show their responses over the course of an entire week. If you could choose one week to experience, whose would you pick? Additionally, for any of these people, which day would you say was the best?

People often have different ways for choosing a week. Some who pick Week A say it's because it allows them to experience the greatest number of positive days and avoid negative ones entirely. Others who pick Week B see value in experiencing both positive and negative days and appreciate its gentle emotional variance. When people choose Week C, some do so because it gets progressively better; others point out that it ends on the highest note. "By the time Saturday rolls around," they say, "you won't remember how you felt on Monday." Others reason that emotions accumulate. When they add up the scores for all seven days, Weeks A and D emerge on top with sums of 7.

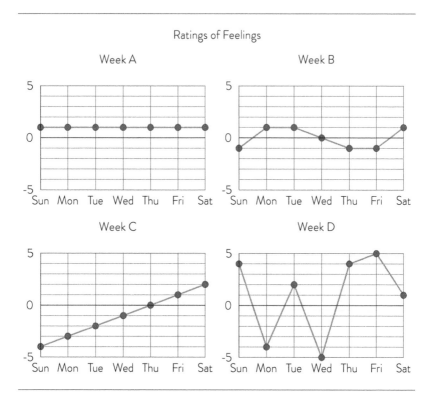

Ratings of Feelings

To break the tie, some people opt for Week D, explaining that they'd rather feel the higher highs...even if it means suffering the lower lows.

When it comes to answering the second question — for a given week, which single day was the best — approaches once again vary. Someone looking at Week D, for instance, might conclude that Friday was the best day, since it had the highest individual rating (+5). However, someone else might suggest that Thursday was actually the best day. Even though it didn't have the highest rating, it did have the highest rating *compared to the day before.* "Since Wednesday was a -5," someone might reason, "then Thursday's score of +4 represents an improvement of +9."

The approach that we take when analyzing feelings is more than a mathematical exercise. It's a philosophical one. In my experience, we in the United States (and in the West more broadly) tend to pursue positive emotions and seek to avoid negative ones. This isn't surprising given the messages that we're exposed to. From commercials showing enthusiastic car buyers to

Instagram selfies of supersaturated smiles, we're surrounded by expressions of positivity. Over time, this can create an expectation that people should strive to experience only those emotions that sit above the x-axis. When our emotions dip into the negative, we're liable to judge ourselves (and others) harshly.

Other cultures and spiritual traditions take a different approach. Rather than view feelings with positive ratings as inherently better than those with negative ones, they view them as mutually dependent. Without down, their reasoning goes, how can there be up? If a person has never endured agony, how can they appreciate bliss? To an emotional relativist, even negative experiences have a silver lining; they accentuate their opposites, much like how Person D's terrible Wednesday made their Thursday even better.

As distinct as these approaches are — valuing the positive only versus valuing the negative *also* — they have an important feature in common: they both distinguish between positive and negative. However, there's another approach that does not. To some people, the defining quality of an emotional experience is not how good or bad it feels but how *intense* it feels.

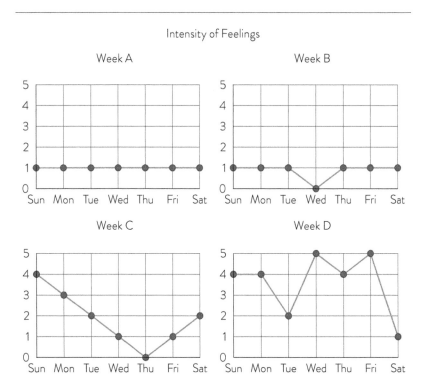

Intensity of Feelings

Someone concerned primarily with the strength of a feeling (rather than the quality of a feeling) will view a day with a rating of +5 and one with a rating of -5 as equivalent; even though their directions are different, their absolute values are the same. When we use this method to evaluate Weeks A, B, C, and D, a new picture emerges. Gone is the separation between pleasure and anger. Dissolved is the distinction between happy and sad. Viewed through the prism of intensity, emotions that we might normally perceive as being opposites are suddenly re-rendered. When someone considers which week they'd rather experience now, the operative question is no longer *how* they want to feel but *how much*. In my experience, most adults choose Weeks A and B, explaining that they no longer have the energy for emotional extremes. Children, on other hand – and middle schoolers in particular – will often opt for Week D. "We want to *feel* life," they say. "We want to feel it *intensely*."

Humans are emotional creatures. With modern technology, it's easier than ever to keep track of how we feel. Angry. Happier. Happiest. Even when we don't assign numbers to our emotions, we're constantly rating them. Since every life involves both easy and difficult days, the emotions we experience will inevitably include both ones that we tend to label as "positive" as well as others that we label as "negative." When we consider the significance of our emotions, though — and in particular, when we treat them as a proxy for how our lives are progressing — the conclusions we draw will have as much to do with how we interpret our feelings as with what those feelings are. It's possible that sadness is an indication that something is wrong and that happiness is a sign that all is right. But it's also possible that such judgements are flawed, and that there's value in embracing the full range of human emotions, from the highest highs to the lowest lows.

Discussion Questions

- If you were to graph your ideal week, what would it look like?

- In general, what is your personal philosophy about so-called "negative" emotions like pain? Are they something to avoid or fix, something to appreciate, or something to feel?

- Imagine someone you know is going through a difficult experience. How might your philosophy influence how you respond?

PART FIVE

PRESERVING THE SOCIAL PURPOSE OF SCHOOL

N 2006, a megamillionaire in California's Silicon Valley launched a new charter school network which he hoped would transform the way children learn. John Danner had earned his fortune by developing technologies to help companies sell ads on the Internet, and his mission with Rocketship Schools was to likewise use technology to improve math instruction. Rocketship would accomplish this by using complex algorithms to "personalize learning" for all of its students, primarily minority children from low-income communities. Software would evaluate their performance in math, then provide each learner with their own tailor-made stream of videos, activities, and assessments to help students progress at their own pace and according to their own interests. The goal of the system, a school administrator explained, was to deliver "the right content to the right kids at the right time, allowing kids to specialize and become proficient."

A centerpiece of Rocketship's model was the network's Learning Lab. For 80 to 100 minutes each day, students were assigned to call-center-like rooms where they donned headphones and worked silently on their computerized lessons. If a student had a question, she couldn't necessarily turn to an experienced teacher for help. Instead, labs were staffed by lower-paid noncertified "supervisors," an arrangement which allowed Rocketship to serve more than 600 children with only six teachers plus aides. Recalling his inaugural experience in a Learning Lab, a former supervisor at Alma Academy in San

Jose described how he'd been left in charge of 90 students on his first day at work. "I didn't know any of their names," he explained. "And it dawns on me later that it wasn't necessarily responsible to leave me like that." As *not-necessarily-responsible* as the school's high-tech approach may have been, it proved effective, at least when it came to improving standardized test scores. Within five years of its founding, Rocketship emerged as one of the highest-performing low-income school systems in California. The network has attracted hundreds of millions of dollars to expand nationwide, and today operates schools in Wisconsin, Tennessee, and Washington, DC.

Yet for all of Rocketship's considerable successes, its emphasis on software-based instruction came with costs. In a 2014 letter to the Santa Clara County school board, Lily Casillas, the mother of a third-grader at Rocketship's Sí Se Puede Academy, described the toll that computerized instruction was taking on her son. "He would get headaches and get tired of focusing too long on the screen," she explained. She recalled her son saying, "I wish there was a teacher instead of looking directly at the computer," and complained that the school's emphasis on standardized testing resulted in her child being "stressed to the point he wanted to throw up." Mrs. Casillas even noted how, in an effort to maximize time in the Learning Labs, school administrators disallowed students from using the bathroom. "Many children are urinating on their pants," she wrote in her letter, and an area pediatrician confirmed that dozens of Rocketship elementary students had been diagnosed with urinary tract infections.

As a curriculum developer, I've written hundreds of questions. But as a citizen, I only have one: *How could this happen?*

...

As with any innovation, personalization operates along a spectrum, and Learning Labs were clearly an extreme. However, they illustrate a larger trend in American education: the increasingly central role that computers are playing in teaching school-aged children. Across the country, a growing number of schools, districts, charter networks, and states have begun to treat algorithms as a core instructional strategy. While they have valid reasons for wanting to do so, when taken too far, the technologization of teaching will undermine the social character of school.

Public education exists for two purposes: to help students develop the knowledge and skills they'll need to succeed in their individual lives, and to create opportunities for children to learn together in order to strengthen our social fabric and ensure a healthy democracy. As math educators, we have an important role to play in each of these.

At this fragile moment in our national history, though — a moment in which our discourse is imperiled by irrationality, incivility, and a lack of critical thought — it is our social contribution that's more urgent than ever. It's also the most threatened by the rise of computerized teaching.

Given the power of mathematics to illuminate everything from homelessness to opioids to the use of force by police officers to the construction of baseball stadiums, we have a unique opportunity to incubate a citizenry committed to reason. If we're to accomplish this, there are a number of hurdles that we must overcome. As we've discussed, we must expand our understanding of what it means for math education to be complete, we must distinguish between looking at math and looking with math, and we must reconsider the justifications that we've historically offered for deprioritizing real-world activities.

However, even if we take all of these steps to transform our classrooms into forums for thoughtful discourse, it will only matter if one thing remains true: we continue to have classrooms in the first place. Students can use mathematics to power conversations about the world around them, but they can only do so if they have someone to converse with. "What's the fairest way for cities to raise revenue?" is a valuable debate for students to have, but they can't have it with an algorithm. This is why the creep of computers in education is so concerning. As we saw with cable news and social media, the personalization of facts may have broken our democracy. The personalization of school may ensure it's never fixed.

This isn't to say that educational software is all bad. There are a number of valid reasons to technologize parts of math instruction, and adaptive software may have a valuable role to play within a broader educational strategy. Schools that pursue personalization aren't necessarily destined to replicate the extremism of Learning Labs, nor are students assigned to devices fated to work on them for hours each day.

But they might. There are a number of powerful forces at work in the United States today that are accelerating the shift towards computerized learning. These forces could combine into a perfect storm that results in human teachers becoming little more than lab assistants and a school day of screen time becoming more the norm than the exception. I realize how hyperbolic this may sound. Unfortunately, not only is this prospect more likely than we may prefer to believe, but it may also arrive sooner than we expect.

The Personalization of Math

Math educators have long attempted to personalize their teaching. If students struggle with fractions, teachers might assign an extra homework packet. If others like sports, they might write word problems involving basketball. However, computers take this process to a whole new level, and there are multiple reasons why educators and others are so interested in incorporating technology into math instruction.

One reason is software's ability to save teachers time. Many of the skills that math educators cover consist of predictable steps, and many of the tasks they assign have closed-ended answers. Instead of asking teachers to walk students through the process of, say, writing a parabola in vertex form — generalizing the equation as $y = a(x-h)^2 + k$; identifying the vertex as (h,k); etc. — and instead of expecting them to allocate hours of instructional time each week to rote practice, advocates of personalized learning argue that these responsibilities can be offloaded to a computer. This is smart. Software is perfectly equipped to scaffold mathematical procedures and evaluate numerical responses.

Not only does the computer absolve teachers of the tedium of grading worksheets, but it also frees up instructional time for higher-order experiences that might not otherwise be feasible. For instance, unlike many real-world activities which can be successfully explored without prior mastery, writing the equation describing the average Major League home run requires a level of fluency with quadratic functions that's only possible towards the end of a unit. The more students can use software to sharpen their mathematical skills outside of the classroom, the more time they'll have to apply these skills in the classroom to debate whether stadiums should be standardized. This is a benefit of software in schools. When educators outsource to technology aspects of the learning experience that computers can handle, they allow themselves to invest more deeply in experiences that only humans can provide.

Another advantage of instructional software is that it allows students to move at their own pace and teachers to monitor their progress. When teaching a skill or concept to a classroom of thirty students, a teacher may have some who have already mastered the material, some who are on track, and others who are struggling. Traditionally, teachers had few options for how to proceed. If they moved on, the struggling students would get discouraged. If they didn't, the advanced ones would get bored.

Personalized learning technology helps resolve this dilemma. If the system determines that students are proficient with a given skill, it can provide them with more challenging questions or advance them to the next topic in the series. If it determines that other students still need work, it can offer additional questions until they're ready to move on. Such adaptations would strain a human teacher, but they're trivial for a computer. On top of that, such technologies often include intuitive dashboards that help teachers follow their students' progress. Under the Common Core, Grade 6 alone consists of 41 separate standards. For a teacher with five sections of thirty students, that's more than 6,000 data points to keep track of. There's no way to do that with an old-fashioned gradebook, but it's easy with adaptive software.

A recent study from RAND found that among teachers whose schools used personalized learning, 17 percent devoted at least a quarter of their class time to working with students one-on-one compared to just 9 percent nationwide. When educators have real-time data about which students are ahead and which are behind, they can tailor their instructional decisions accordingly. This matters. One of the thorniest questions in American education is whether or not to "track" students by ability: directing advanced students to the honors track, struggling students to the remedial track, and everyone else to the standard track. One of the main arguments against tracking is that, since assignments are often made in elementary school, and since students' performance in math at that age is highly correlated to parental income, it inadvertently perpetuates a cycle in which privileged students move farther ahead while less affluent ones fall farther behind. The more adaptive software can help educators differentiate instruction to students of varying abilities in the same class, the more it may help to correct some of the institutional inequities that have long plagued American education.

A third reason that many educators value computerized instruction is that it addresses gaps in teacher knowledge and allows schools to offer courses for which they wouldn't otherwise have the resources. Even among experienced educators, mathematical content knowledge can vary widely. If you've been teaching for long enough, you've likely encountered some colleagues with an expert-level understanding of math and others who seemed to know no math at all.

There are various explanations for the latter. In middle school, it's often because teachers are working beyond their competency or experience. When states adopted the Common Core Standards, for instance, a number of topics that were traditionally taught in high school algebra were moved to eighth grade, meaning that educators with middle school licenses were suddenly working out of scope. In Georgia, only 7 percent of elementary teachers said that they felt comfortable with their new standards' emphasis on conceptual understanding and problem solving, compared to their original standards' focus on procedures.

For a principal in this position, an adaptive program to personalize skill development can seem like a useful backstop. "Even if I wouldn't normally want students to work independently on a computer," an administrator might reason, "at least this way I'm raising the floor."

Not only can instructional software address shortcomings in schools' existing courses, it also allows administrators to offer courses that they might not be able to otherwise. In rural areas, low student enrollment and teacher shortages can make it infeasible for high schools to offer subjects like statistics or calculus. Khan Academy addresses everything from preschool math to multi-variable calculus. Even if a principal can't hire a human teacher to teach differential equations, they can still get Sal.

Just as an iPad app for piano scales can play a useful role in a child's musical development, it seems reasonable that instructional software that helps students practice skills and explore concepts can be an important part of a student's mathematical experience. The key, of course, is *part*. Computerized teaching may be worth incorporating into math instruction, but only as one piece of a larger mosaic. As math educators, we can help students think critically and help them graduate into the world as more curious and respectful citizens. If we're to accomplish this, it is absolutely critical that our classrooms remain centers for shared learning experiences and not be simply converted into glorified computer labs.

However, there are three forces in the United States which, when combined, I fear could cause personalized learning software to assume a much larger role than it should.

Force 1: The Slippery Slope of Technology

When John Danner started Rocketship, I doubt he foresaw that eight-year-olds would one day go dizzy from staring at screens or be scolded for using the bathroom. Danner wasn't some ignorant amateur who parachuted into education. After earning his fortune, he got a master's degree in education policy and then worked as an elementary school teacher in Nashville, Tennessee. But that's the thing about technology: it often starts out innocuously enough, then takes on a life of its own. When Apple introduced the iPhone in 2007, it was billed as a convenient way to send email and navigate around town. Now smartphones are the first things we look at when we wake up, the last things we touch before we go to bed, and devices without which many could not imagine existing.

A school administrator who reads about Learning Labs might think, "That would never happen to us. We'd never let it go that far." But when it comes to technology, it can be a slippery slope from inclusion to dependency, from adoption to addiction.

From what I've observed, there are two traps that schools and districts regularly fall into when incorporating educational technology. The first is the "money trap." An institution makes a large initial investment in something like devices or personalized learning. Having spent a significant sum to adopt the new technology, they feel obliged to continue to support it, even if it doesn't pan out.

In 2013, the Los Angeles Unified School District launched a $1.3 billion initiative to provide every student in the city with an iPad. Only after Apple had delivered 75,000 devices did district officials discover that the digital curriculum installed on them didn't work. Instead of canceling the program, they invested an additional $40 million to salvage it. Behavioral economists refer to this as the "sunk cost fallacy." Your car breaks down so you pay to have the transmission replaced. Then the brakes fail, the fuel pump dies, and the radiator explodes. Rather than scrap the car, you tell the mechanic to fix everything. After all, you already paid for the transmission!

In the United States, the median-sized school district consists of six schools and 15,000 students. Imagine one such district decided to launch personalized learning in all of its math classes. First it has to buy the software. If administrators are content with YouTube lectures and multiple-choice quizzes, they can use Khan Academy for free. But if they need something more robust, an advanced program like DreamBox — in my opinion one of the highest-quality options for online skills development — can cost upwards of $7,000 per school. Then there are the devices. If the district provides every student with their own $300 Chromebook laptop, it will cost just over $4.5 million. Even if it opts for classroom sets, though, it will still spend hundreds of thousands of dollars. On top of this, administrators may need to upgrade their bandwidth, train teachers on the new technology, and even reschedule classes. When all is said and done, what sounds like a straightforward initiative to "adopt personalized learning" may cost millions of dollars and require many system-wide changes.

And so what happens if it doesn't work out? If teachers end up determining that personalized learning is ineffective, will the district cut its losses and move on to something else? Maybe. But maybe not. Investments like these involve powerful players, from the local school board to the superintendent. After investing so much money, how eager would they be to admit that it was all for naught? Rather than cancel the program, they may decide to double down, digging themselves deeper into the money pit...and making it harder to ever get out. After all, every dollar that a school spends on technology is a dollar that it can't spend on professional development, high-quality curriculum, or other more human-centric resources. The more schools invest in computers, then, the more they may come to rely on them.

The second trap that schools and districts sometimes fall into when adopting educational technology is the "framework trap." Administrators start out by adopting the system needed to technologize part of the learning experience...but gradually come to treat it as a filter for the *entire* learning experience. This is something that many of us do in our personal lives, albeit for lower stakes. I own an Amazon Kindle. When I originally bought the e-reader more than a decade ago, I only planned to use it when I traveled; I wanted to fly with multiple books without having to carry the weight. Today, though, if a book is not available for the Kindle, I don't even consider reading it.

In the same way, school administrators may initially adopt a technology with a narrow use case in mind, but eventually come to treat it as a factor in larger decisions. Imagine a high school wants to make it easier for students to submit essays and practice math skills at home, so it purchases laptops for all of its students. A year later, the math department informs administrators that it needs a new algebra curriculum and is debating between a highly rated print-based curriculum and a less-effective digital alternative. Which do you expect the school will choose? When viewed through the lens of instruction, the choice is clear; adopt the superior resource regardless of its format. But when viewed through the lens of laptops, decision making becomes highly distorted.

The head of a charter school once told me that his teachers had considered incorporating Citizen Math lessons into their curriculum, but that school administrators had nixed the idea. The reason, he explained, was that the school had just installed a complex computer system to track student progress and could only consider resources that "generated student data." According to its mission statement, the school was founded specifically to prepare students to become "*active citizens.*" Nonetheless, school leadership determined that they couldn't use *Citizen Math* because our lessons weren't compatible with their computer system. When the school head told me this, I couldn't help but laugh. I felt like I was in the middle of an educational hybrid of a Franz Kafka novel and an Abbott and Costello routine.

Yet as absurd as this decision may seem, it's not surprising when you consider how slippery the slope of educational technology can be. An institution adopts a device or software program in an attempt to improve part of what it does...then allows the technology to determine *everything* it does.

On Khan Academy, users receive points for watching videos and completing exercises. Students who collect 10 million points receive the coveted Black Hole Badge. The name is fitting and an apt metaphor for a broader phenomenon. When schools adopt a technology like computer-based teaching, they often do so with the intention of using it in a narrow and well-defined way, then gradually slide into a chasm that they didn't foresee and may not escape. Math teachers have students use iPads to practice rote skills during the last ten minutes of class, and eventually the principal is building a computer lab to "personalize learning." This isn't bound to happen, of course. But it can, imperceptibly and unintentionally.

As educators in America, we have a history of slippery slopes: of allowing a small thing to become a big thing, then the big thing to become the whole thing. We did it with accountability and standardized testing. We could do it again with personalized learning. In Rhode Island, the state board of education's strategic plan specifically calls for "digital opportunities that provide students the ability to control the pace, space, and content of their learning." In Utah, "new school system models for personalized learning implementation." In Mississippi, "innovative programs to improve student outcomes, [including] online and personalized learning." Rocketship Learning Labs may seem like an extreme case of technology run amok. But once mainstream education has accepted the premise that screen time is a necessary component of learning math, 100 minutes per day is merely a matter of degree. This sounds alarmist, I know. Then again, so did early warnings about smartphone addiction.

Force 2: Budget Shortfalls and Tech Philanthropists

In April 2020, as businesses nationwide closed due to the coronavirus pandemic, school superintendents from 62 cities wrote a letter to Congress describing the dire financial situation they faced. "40 to 50 percent of school district revenue comes from local sources that are expected to drop precipitously," they warned. "Dark clouds are forming on the educational horizon." Leaders in California projected that they could cut up to a fifth of their school funding. Ohio slashed its education budget by $300 million, while New York cut its by more than $1 billion. In their letter, the superintendents estimated that 275,000 teachers could be laid off in their cities alone.

The underfunding of American education did not begin with COVID. When the housing market began to collapse in 2007, so did the property taxes that fund local schools. Educators are accustomed to the poverty that characterizes American schooling and prevents them from building attractive facilities, compensating teachers adequately, and investing in quality instructional materials. This isn't new.

What is new is the role that tech philanthropists are playing in filling these financial gaps and accelerating the pace of the digitization of schooling. Every year, charitable foundations such as the Gates Foundation provide billions of dollars' worth of grants to schools, districts, and charter networks around the country. When they do this, they don't simply allocate money for schools to spend as they wish. Instead, a foundation will typically issue a grant for a specific purpose, then invite educators to apply. One of the main priorities today is the adoption of personalized learning. In 2014, a consortium of philanthropies awarded $450,000 to a middle school in Alabama to support the transition to self-directed learning. A year later, it provided grants of $300,000 to schools in New Orleans to provide students with laptops and adaptive math software. In 2018, Chicago Public Schools received a whopping $14 million to install personalized learning technology in schools throughout the city.

For schools and districts who were already planning to use technology to individualize instruction, grants like these can be wonderfully helpful. For others, though, they can seem coercive, and can put them in a position to make instructional decisions that, if they weren't so cash-strapped, they'd otherwise avoid. The problem isn't that philanthropists are providing financial support. The problem, in my opinion, is that they're naturally prioritizing what they know...and what they know is technology. Consider who some of the most prominent funders are and how they earned their fortunes:

- Bill and Melinda Gates Foundation (Microsoft)
- Chan-Zuckerberg Initiative (Facebook)
- Hewlett Foundation (Hewlett-Packard)
- Michael and Susan Dell Foundation (Dell Computers)
- Verizon Foundation (Verizon)
- Google.org (Google)

Given that many of today's most powerful philanthropists earned their fortunes in technology, it makes sense that they'd view education through computer-colored glasses. Recalling a visit he once made to a school where he observed students working silently on laptops and progressing at their own pace, Facebook founder Mark Zuckerberg mused, "When you visit a school like this, it feels like the future. You get the feeling this is how more of the education system should work." Given his background, it's not surprising that he would think this, and maybe he's right. Maybe school-by-software is the future.

But hopefully not.

The purpose of school is to create opportunities for children to interact with and learn from one another. Classrooms are spaces for students to think deeply about the world, to consider issues from multiple perspectives, and to learn how to communicate clearly and rigorously. Facebook, on the other hand, reaffirms what users already believe by tailoring posts and news articles to their personal beliefs. Twitter limits comments to a few dozen characters. Emojis replace nuanced expression with hieroglyphics. And the ceaseless cacophony of smartphone notifications obliterates our attention spans. In many ways, the innovations that have allowed tech philanthropists to assume such an outsized role in shaping the direction of American education aren't just inconsistent with school; they're antithetical to it. They exacerbate exactly the problems that school is intended to solve. Relying on Silicon Valley billionaires to transform teaching and learning, then, is a bit like asking the Marlboro Man to cure cancer.

Technologists are free to describe computers and algorithms as the "future" of education (just as they're free to define staring silently at a screen as "social" media). But as actual educators we should consider whether theirs is a vision we share and whether the utopia of individualization that they fantasize about is the reality we want to create.

Still, school budgets *have* been decimated, and school administrators *are* under tremendous pressure to find money wherever they can. This is the reality facing educators throughout the country. The Gates Foundation and the Chan-Zuckerberg Initiative alone have a combined endowment of almost $60 billion. That's a lot of gravity. Indeed, it's more than the annual educational expenditure of every state in the country except for New York and California. This is the second reason why the extreme case of a Learning Lab may become more ubiquitous than many of us assume and why a shift to algorithm-as-teacher may happen sooner than we expect. It isn't that educators are necessarily enamored with the idea of going all-in on computerized instruction. It's that many philanthropists are. They seek to recreate school in their pixelated image, and they're willing to write the check to do it.

Force 3: American Individualism

At its core, the United States is an individual-oriented country. Our founding was a literal declaration of independence. Individualism is central to our DNA. You can hear it in the call that inspired farmers to cross the plains: "Go west, young man." You can see it in the old westerns about cowboys riding solo across the range and in every car ad urging drivers to flee the crowded city along solitary stretches of asphalt. Even our heroes are singular: Super*man*, Wonder *Woman*, the *Lone* Ranger, and a *personal* Jesus.

This isn't to say that we don't have collective identities. We do. We associate with political parties. We cheer for our favorite sports teams. During the Second World War, we rallied to ration sugar, buy war bonds, and rosily rivet B-24s. Nor is it to say that our independent spirit is bad. I can't imagine that Elvis would have invented rock and roll anywhere other than the American South. Tesla founder Elon Musk may have been *born* in South Africa but he was *made* in California.

Still, independence is what defines us. The system of national parks we share may be America's *best idea*, but the American *dream* remains a single-family home surrounded by a fence. If individualized housing is where we choose to live, then individualized teaching may be how we choose to learn. When we consider the likelihood that students in the United States will one day spend much of their time working in cubicles on a computer, we cannot separate our tolerance for individualization from the prevailing cultural zeitgeist. While school exists to improve society, it's also a reflection of it.

The Dangers of Personalization

Proponents of adaptive learning software advertise it as a *strategy*. They describe it as a *tool*, something that exists to solve a narrow problem: students not knowing their times tables, for instance, or needing extra practice for standardized tests. In fact, personalization is far more than a technology. It's an ideology. The algorithmically-powered individualization of teaching is the manifestation of the belief that learning should be digitized and that the purpose of school is to serve the individual alone. Personalization is not a product. It's a dogma.

And it's a dogma that's come to dominate not just the educational landscape but much of our human experience more broadly. We are surrounded today by the doctrine of individualization. You can see it in Netflix, which analyzes our viewing history to personalize the movies its recommends that we watch. You can see it on Amazon, which uses our book purchases to suggest new novels for us to read.

Sometimes this personalization can be helpful. On Spotify, a country music fan who listens to Lyle Lovett will be introduced to other similar artists. That's great. On the other hand, computer-powered individualization can be limiting. For while Spotify's recommendation algorithm will expose a country music fan to Alison Krauss and Brandi Carlile, it won't expose him to Caetano Veloso, Depeche Mode, the Eurythmics, Fairuz, Gift of Gab, Hombres G, the Indigo Girls, Jackson 5, Kendrick Lamar, Lord T & Eloise, Mozart, Nirvana, Ozomatli, Pink Floyd, Queen, Ravi Shankar, Sigur Rós, Tribe Called Quest, UB40, Van Morrison, or Wham. Spotify may recommend Yonder Mountain String Band and ZZ Top; those are pretty close to country. But it won't suggest Yo-Yo Ma or Zap Mama. As long as country-western is the filter, artists like them might as well not even exist.

Of course, as valuable as it may be for people to be exposed to more than just a narrow sliver of the artistic spectrum, I suppose it doesn't really matter what movies individuals watch, what photos they look at, or what songs they hear. However, the computer-powered individualization of our digital lives isn't limited to entertainment. It applies to information as well. And this is where personalization goes from being culturally limiting to societally destructive.

On YouTube, a user who starts out watching a clip questioning whether Lee Harvey Oswald assassinated JFK is gradually pulled into a wormhole where 9/11 was a hoax, Sandy Hook didn't happen, vaccines cause autism, the Democratic Party is a pedophilia cult, and the moon landing was filmed on a sound stage in Hollywood. Today, a third of millennials believe the Earth may be flat. It isn't, but inaccuracy isn't a deal-breaker for the video recommendation algorithms that power YouTube.

In 2018, an internal Facebook report revealed that in 64 percent of cases in which a user joined an extremist group, Facebook's algorithm had suggested it. This included at least three dozen groups dedicated to denying the Holocaust. In Europe, the tragedy happened. Until October 2020, when Facebook explicitly banned Holocaust denial, its existence was up to users. At any given moment, roughly 570,000 people in the United States are experiencing homelessness. If homelessness isn't an issue that Facebook deems "relevant" to users, though, will they ever hear about it?

As a country, we are more divided today that we've been in a generation. Our discourse is unmoored from reason and driven largely by emotion. A 2017 study from the Johns Hopkins School of Health concluded that the more time we spend on social media, the less happy we are. And while the challenges we face are becoming more urgent by the day — climate change, the coronavirus pandemic, wealth inequality, political extremism — our prospects for resolving them are only becoming less likely.

Of course, this isn't the fault of companies like Google, Facebook, and the myriad others whose fortunes are built atop personalization algorithms. They didn't invent divisiveness. But they do accelerate it. Humans have an innate desire to feel secure, and there's nothing more comforting than a reflection of reality that confirms what we already believe. By manipulating our psychology for their profitable ends, the priests of individualization have accelerated a social cleaving which may prove unbridgeable. If American democracy is to succeed, then we as citizens must ground our discourse in a common understanding of reality. But how can we do that if we don't agree on what reality is?

Public education operates within a larger social context. And much of that context has become defined (and constrained) by the philosophy of personalization. Before we incorporate individualized learning technologies into our schools, then, we would be wise to consider the effects that individualization has had on modern life more broadly. From social isolation to technological addiction, conspiracy theories to partisan tribalism, many of the problems that we're suffering as a nation (indeed as a species) are worsened by the algorithms we use and the dogma that underlies them: that every user should be the arbiter of their own personal truth, and that an individualized reality is the truest expression of human engagement.

As educators, is this the ideology that we want to define how children learn? Are algorthmically-generated tailor-made pathways that "adapt to students' actions" the truest articulation of the future of our profession...or are they exactly the prospect we ought to avoid?

As you read this, the companies who develop adaptive learning systems are hard at work improving their products and making them more powerful. Personalized learning technologies will only get better and the leaps between them will only come faster. Who knows; maybe soon enough a child will be able to don a virtual reality headset in kindergarten and not remove it until high school graduation.

Just because a technology exists to digitize teaching, though, doesn't mean we have to adopt it. *Every student for himself* is not a fate. It's a choice. And it's a choice that we don't have to make.

The Importance of Social Learning

I had an interesting conversation with my 70-something-year-old mom recently about exercise. Normally she attends the Body Pump class at the local gym. But since the outbreak of the coronavirus, she hasn't done group fitness. Instead, she's been going to the neighbors' house to use their Peloton, a stationary bike equipped with a screen that allows riders to join workouts remotely. The app allows users to compare their performance to others' in the class and provides real-time data and personalized tips. I asked my mom how she was liking it. "It's great," she replied, marveling at the range of additional services that Peloton offers. "They have yoga. They have stretching. They have weights. They have everything." But then she paused to rethink. "The bike is very convenient," she said, "but when I use it, I'm in a basement by myself. I'd rather work out with other people."

It's possible to exercise on your own. It's even possible to use software to simulate a group activity. And yet no matter how advanced the technology becomes, exercising alone cannot replace the camaraderie of exercising together. We humans are social animals. We can download all the apps that we want, but nothing can replicate the experience of turning to someone who's gasping for breath, looking them in the eye, and saying, "You've got this."

The same is true of education. Learning is a social process. Schools and classrooms are settings for social interactions. Public education is a system for strengthening society. While computerized individualization may have a role to play in some aspects of learning, the aspects that we tend to value most require other people. We want students to learn how to share. For this to happen, they need someone to share with. We want students to learn how to articulate their reasoning. For that to happen, they need someone to articulate it to. From Facebook to YouTube, Netflix to Spotify, the technologies that power modern life today effectively place every user at the center of their own universe. Not surprisingly, this is exactly what the developers of personalized-learning software promise to do for students. Yet while this may be an efficient way for students to get better at times tables, when it comes to the qualities like humility, empathy, patience, kindness, and the consideration of opposing viewpoints, these all require social interaction. They cannot be individualized.

Given the centrality of interaction to the human learning process, it may seem crazy that we're even considering digitizing it. From what I can tell, the reason that educators and others have become so enthusiastic about the prospect of personalized learning is the same reason that my mother uses the

Peloton: it's convenient. Millions of students are behind grade level in math. Their fluency is weak. Their understanding is thin. Faced with high-stakes standardized tests, school officials are understandably desperate for a solution that fills these gaps, preferably as quickly and conveniently as possible. This is exactly what adaptive learning software purports to do. And if it works, great.

But we have to be careful about convenience. Once upon a time we bought meat from the butcher, bread from the baker, and milk from the dairy farmer. Our shopping was social but it took hours to do. So we transitioned to mom and pop grocery stores that stocked our basic staples...then to supermarkets that stocked everything else...then to Target...and eventually to Amazon. With the click of a button, we can now have everything we need delivered to our doorstep with minimal effort and zero interactions. Is this more convenient? Yes. But is it better?

Let me ask you: the hatred that we spout on social media; the impatience we exhibit towards with those who think differently; the reactive sensitivities that so often explode into apoplexy. Do you think the anger that characterizes so much of our culture today exists because we substantively disagree about the issues we face, or is it that we've simply forgotten how to interact? Are we so divided as a country because we legitimately view policies like the minimum wage and mask mandates differently? Or are we simply grasping at partisanship because it's *something* to grab onto, because we've become so removed from one another and have come to occupy such lonely bubbles that we're desperate for connection — any type of connection — even if it's a connection defined by opposition? These aren't rhetorical questions. The grocery apps that require no social interaction. The streaming services that allow us to skip the line at the movie theater. The ride-sharing apps that make it easy to arrive alone by car rather than with others on the bus. All of these technologies make our lives more convenient, but do they make our lives better? Do they make us better? Or are they Faustian bargains that are digitally eroding the best part of being human, namely: being human *together*?

In this era of loneliness and societal fragmentation, I believe that school represents our last best hope as a country. It's the place where children can discover how to work together and learn from one another. School is a setting for coexistence. Indeed, this is one of the main reasons that we as a society built public schools in the first place, and why we require students to spend on average seven hours a day 180 days a year in them. If we've already created the infrastructure and fueled the buses that deliver students to the school building, why would we want to put them on computers as soon as they arrive?

In my opinion, the euphoria that many feel for the computer-based individualization of education (and math education in particular) is preposterous. From speeding tickets to coupons, stadium construction to the acceleration of human innovation, math class represents a unique opportunity for students to think critically about real issues in the world and to consider them from multiple perspectives. If a student is to view reality from an angle other than her own, she first needs to be in an environment with someone other than herself. Of course, it's possible for this environment to be a chat room. Students could discuss opioids and homelessness via keyboard and computer screen. But why? Learning is a social process. Why would we want to digitize it?

Signs of Hope

Technologies like adaptive learning software offer benefits, and there may be some aspects of the mathematical experience that are worth personalizing. The more schools and districts come to incorporate these technologies, though, the more careful they'll need to be about their overuse, and the more diligent we as educators need to be about make sure we're not complicit in the erosion of our profession. Computer-based teaching is by definition an anti-social endeavor that when taken too far undermines the communal spirit of public education. We're still in the early days, but the dangers of high-tech personalization are real. For once the soul of school is gone, it may be gone for good. Fortunately there's hope. For all the central office administrators, policymakers, and educational philanthropists who are clamoring to hasten the technologization of American schooling, there's another group of people who are beginning to push back: students themselves.

In November 2018, a group of high schoolers in Brooklyn walked out of school. Their administrators had recently adopted a computer-based personalized learning curriculum, and students were exhausted from spending up to five hours each day staring at screens. In an open letter, students explained their decision. "[We] feel as if [we] are not learning anything," they wrote. "The entire program eliminates much of the human interaction, teacher support, and discussion and debate with our peers that we need in order to improve our critical thinking."

In addition to the social erosion, students also took issue with the way that personalized learning is treated differently in low-income schools than in wealthy ones. "There is a huge class divide," they wrote, "with the children of the wealthy having small classes and real personalized learning in schools that minimize screen time, while public school students like us are expected to learn by a computer in front of our faces for hours at a time with educators only there to 'facilitate.'"

The students in Brooklyn weren't alone. In the small town of McPherson, Kansas, two months later, another group of students staged a walkout in response to tech-based personalization. They described spending so much time doing digital lessons each day that they got headaches and hand cramps. "We're allowing the computers to teach the kids," complained the father of a fourth-grader. "And the kids all looked like zombies." A tenth-grader was equally exasperated with her technologized teaching. "I want to just take my Chromebook back and tell them I'm not doing it anymore."

In response to the criticism, the developer of the online curriculum explained that it never intended for students to spend so much time each day learning by computer. The problem, it explained, was that school administrators had simply implemented the product incorrectly, and so they dispatched trainers nationwide to clarify best practices. Even if user error was to blame, the episode highlights how easy it is for schools that adopt tech-based teaching to descend down a slippery slope. It also spotlights a truth that many techtopians would prefer to ignore: that "personalized" learning can be awfully impersonal.

Of course, it isn't just students in Brooklyn and Kansas who understand the limitations of educational technology. Suddenly we all do. In the spring of 2020, schools across the United States began to close in response to the coronavirus pandemic, shifting from in-person learning to remote learning. In some cases students did the same activities with their teachers that they would have otherwise, just by video conference instead of in the classroom. In other cases students were assigned to full-scale online learning programs where the software became the teacher. Whatever approach schools took, millions of American students, teachers, and families got their first taste of school-by-computer.

The taste has been decidedly sour. According to pediatricians and child psychologists, the experience of remote learning has left many children isolated and depressed. According to a survey conducted roughly seven months after school lockdowns began, more than half of U.S. students say they're worried about their mental health, and nearly a quarter of high schoolers know someone who's considered suicide. Describing her frustration with learning remotely, a 16 year-old in Maryland observed, "I used to complain every day about having to go to school, but being in quarantine has really made me appreciate being in class." A 9 year-old in Los Angeles was even more succinct. "I'm hoping that things will be back to normal someday." For all the bright-eyed promises about the virtues of online learning, the school closures sparked by COVID-19 reveal a starkly different picture: a digital wasteland of educational solitude.

The pandemic has been awful. It's cost hundreds of thousands of lives. It's erased millions of jobs. It's siloed children in bedrooms and alienated them from their teachers and friends. And yet for everything that the virus has stolen, it's offered a rare gift: an opportunity to consider whether the technologization of American schooling is really something we want to pursue. There's something poetic in this. A vaccine works by exposing the body to a small dose of the illness. By forcing us to shutter classrooms and experience first-hand what it's like to learn by computer, the pandemic may have inadvertently inoculated us against the infected ideology of digital schooling and a future of learning alone.

I hope so. But we'll have to stay vigilant. In May 2020, as schools across New York began to close in response to the coronavirus, governor Andrew Cuomo met with Microsoft founder Bill Gates and former Google CEO Eric Schmidt to discuss the possibilities for online learning. After the meeting, the governor marveled at their vision for education. "All these buildings," he said, gesturing to the nearly 5,000 schools spread out across his state. "All these physical classrooms. Why, with all the technology [we] have?"

As a citizen, you may recoil when you hear about students being herded into a computer lab and spending so much time on instructional software each day that they barely have time to interacte and go dizzy from staring at screens. If you're anything like me, you might wonder, "How could this possibly happen?"

It happens exactly like this: with someone in a position of power looking at a classroom and concluding that it's obsolete.

MATHEMATICAL VIGNETTE

HEALTH INSURANCE MARKETS

How should we organize a health insurance market?

mathematics used: percents, expected value

To buy health insurance or not to buy health insurance? It's a question that countless Americans face each year. It's also a question that in 2009 sparked acerbic and occasionally violent town hall meetings across the country, and which we as a population haven't gotten much better at discussing since. Access to medical care is an incredibly important issue. If we're to successfully address the challenges facing our health care system, we must first understand how health insurance works, including the various proposals for how to improve it.

As vitriolic as the health insurance debate has been in the United States, though, insurance itself is a fairly simple concept. Insurance is basically a mechanism for sharing risk. In an insurance market, people come together and contribute a certain amount of money (called a "premium") to a pot. If anyone gets sick or injured, money from the pot is used to pay their medical bills. By pooling their money, participants are able to receive care that they might not be able to afford on their own. When someone purchases a health insurance policy, they effectively agree to share their risk with others in exchange for accepting others' risk in return. In a sense, signing up for insurance is like joining the Three Musketeers: *all for one and one for all.*

But the Musketeers comparison isn't entirely accurate. For even though everyone who buys insurance receives the protection it provides, not everyone will end up needing it. In fact, an insurance market can only succeed if most participants *don't get sick*. And therein lies the rub. An insurance market depends on lots of people participating, but people will only participate if they think insurance is worth the price. And to some, it won't be worth the price. It can't be.

To understand why, let's consider a simple scenario (and an admittedly unrealistic one). Imagine a country with just four residents and one medical procedure: a $40,000 heart surgery. The residents vary in age and health status, and each has a different probability of having a heart attack — and thus needing the surgery — in a given year. Based on their risk profiles, who do you expect would value insurance the most, and who do you expect would value it the least?

Resident	Alonso	Beatriz	Claire	Daniel
Probability of Needing Surgery in a Given Year	1%	16%	25%	50%

Since Daniel is the most likely to get sick, insurance is worth the most to him. Since Alonso is the least likely, insurance is worth the least. The values for Beatriz and Claire are somewhere in between.

This may seem intuitive; the more likely someone is to need insurance, the more it's worth. But how much is insurance worth to each resident *specifically*? If a heart surgery costs $40,000, how much should each person be willing to pay for a policy that covers it?

To answer this, economists calculate an "expected value." If Alonso didn't have insurance, then in any given year he'd have a 1% probability of having to spend $40,000 on surgery and a 99% probability of having to spend zero. His expected value of insurance, then, is (0.01 · $40,000) + (0.99 · $0) = $400. According to economists, Alonso should be willing to pay $400 to avoid the *possibility* of paying $40,000.

So what about Beatriz, Claire, and Daniel? Since they're all at greater risk of a heart attack than Alonso is, they all have higher expected values of insurance. When we calculate the value for every resident, we find that — as expected — the more likely someone is to get sick, the more valuable insurance becomes.

In this sense, buying insurance is similar to playing the lottery; the bigger the jackpot is and the more likely someone is to win, the more they should be willing to spend on a ticket. The difference with insurance is that instead of paying to *take a chance*, a customer is paying to *not*.

	Alonso	Beatriz	Claire	Daniel
Price of Surgery	$40,000	$40,000	$40,000	$40,000
Probability of Surgery	1%	16%	25%	50%
Expected Value of Insurance	$400	$6,400	$10,000	$20,000

The expected values represent how much each resident should be *willing* to pay for a health care policy. But how much will they *actually* pay? This is where the insurance company comes in. One might assume that the company would charge everyone a different price based on their health, but it won't. In many countries (including the United States), insurance companies are required to charge everyone the same price for a given policy. In our hypothetical country, then, what will this single price be?

When someone purchases a health care plan, they shift the financial risk of medical care from themselves to the insurance company. To a customer, insurance offers an expected value. To the company selling it, it represents an expected cost.

If all four people bought insurance, then the company would assume a total expected liability of $400 + $6,400 + $10,000 + $20,000 = $36,800. (Of course, there's no way for the company to actually spend this amount on surgeries. It can only spend a multiple of $40,000, from $0 if nobody gets sick to $160,000 if everyone does. When the company considers the *probability* of each outcome, though, it comes up with an *expected* cost of $36,800 from covering all four residents.)

Based on this, if the company is required to charge everyone the same price — and for simplicity, assuming it only needs to break even and not earn a profit — then it will charge $36,800 ÷ 4, or $9,200 per year.

Now that we know both how much insurance will cost and how much it's worth to each resident, the fun can begin. We can experiment with different options for structuring an insurance market and see how they play out over time...including the options that Congress was considering in 2009 when debating the Affordable Care Act.

Option 1: Allow Everyone to Decide Whether to Buy Insurance

The first option for structuring an insurance market is to allow individuals to decide for themselves whether or not to purchase a policy. If the government of our four-person country chooses this option, how will it play out?

At $9,200, insurance costs more than it's worth to Alonso (who values insurance at $400) and Beatriz (who values it at $6,000). Therefore they won't buy it. On the other hand, Claire and Daniel will, since insurance costs less than their expected values ($10,000 and $20,000, respectively).

Even though the uninsured Alonso and Beatriz are now at risk of paying fullprice for surgery, it's a risk they're willing to take. However, the outcome puts the insurance company in an awkward position. By selling two policies at $9,200 each, the company collects $18,400 from Claire and Daniel...but it expects to spend $30,000 on their surgeries. From the company's perspective, the first year of the insurance market constitutes an unacceptably high risk. So what will it do?

It'll increase the price of insurance before the start of the second year. Specifically, with $30,000 in expected liabilities from the two customers in the pool, it'll raise the price of a policy to $15,000 per year. When it does, though, the price of insurance suddenly exceeds Claire's expected value. As a result, she'll cancel her policy, leaving only Daniel and his $20,000 valuation. Just as in the first year, the company will collect less in premiums than it expects to spend on surgery.

Before the start of the third year, then, it'll raise the price of insurance again, this time to $20,000. At this price, Daniel is — in the language of economics — *indifferent* to buying it. Assuming he decides to (and assuming he can still afford to), by Year 3 the market has become stable. Insurance will continue to cost $20,000 each year, and Daniel will forever remain the only person in the pool.

The cycle of increasing prices and decreasing enrollments that we just observed is common in areas where individuals are allowed to decide for

Buy Insurance or Not	Alonso (EV = $400)	Beatriz (EV = $6,400)	Claire (EV = $10,000)	Daniel (EV = $20,000)
Year 1: Price = $9,200	✗	✗	✓	✓
Year 2: Price = $15,000	✗	✗	✗	✓
Year 3: Price = $20,000	✗	✗	✗	✓

themselves whether or not to join the insurance pool. Many low-risk people opt not to buy insurance...leaving only higher-risk customers in the pool...causing the price of insurance to go up...prompting even more people to drop out. In fact, this cycle is so common that it even has a name: the death spiral. And yet as ominous as this description sounds, there's an upside to an insurance system that prioritizes personal liberty: nobody is forced to buy something that they don't want.

At the same time, there's also a downside: a large fraction of the country is uninsured and exposed to costly (and potentially bankrupting) medical bills. This isn't just dangerous for people who don't have insurance. It's also risky for those who do. If any of the uninsured Alonso, Beatriz, or Claire has a heart attack, the hospital will still treat them; it has an obligation to do so. But if they can't pay its $40,000 bill, the hospital will try to recoup its loss by raising the price of surgery...which in turn will cause the price of insurance to go up.

Option 2: Allow the Insurance Company to Deny Coverage for Preexisting Conditions

Alonso, Beatriz, and Claire decided not to buy insurance because they found it too expensive. A major reason why was Daniel. Because the insurance company expected to spend so much on his medical care, his participation in the pool elevated the price for everyone else. So what would happen if the insurance company didn't cover him? If you were looking closely, you may have noticed a scar on Daniel's chest. If the insurance company were allowed to deny coverage based on Daniel's "pre-existing condition," would that prevent the market from descending into a death spiral? Let's find out.

Now that the insurance company only has to account for Alonso, Beatriz, and Claire, it can calculate a new expected liability: $400 + $6,400 + $10,000 = $16,800. To break even now, the company only has to charge an annual price of $16,800 ÷ 3 = $5,600. This is cheaper than the $9,200 from before.

But it isn't cheap enough for everyone. Even at this lower price, Alonso opts out of the insurance pool, while Beatriz and Claire join it. Once again, this puts the insurance company in an untenable position. In the market's first year, the company collects $11,200 from its two customers' premiums but expects to spend $16,400 on their surgeries. Like before, the company will increase the price of a policy, this time to $8,200...causing Beatriz to drop out...and leaving only Claire. By the third year, the market will be stable with Claire paying $10,000 each year for insurance.

Buy Insurance or Not	Alonso (EV = $400)	Beatriz (EV = $6,400)	Claire (EV = $10,000)	Daniel (EV = n/a)
Year 1: Price = $5,600	✗	✓	✓	✗
Year 2: Price = $8,200	✗	✗	✓	✗
Year 3: Price = $10,000	✗	✗	✓	✗

So is this situation preferable to the previous one? On one hand, excluding Daniel from the insurance pool did cause the long-term price to come down (from $20,000 to $10,000). On the other hand, since the highest-risk resident is no longer covered by insurance, there's an even greater chance that hospitals will be forced to provide uncompensated care. Either way, though, these are just details. When the government allows the insurance company to deny coverage based on a pre-existing condition, it does change how the outcome *looks*. But it doesn't change what the outcome *is*. In the end, the death spiral still happened, and 75% of the country was once again left uninsured.

Option 3: Require Everyone to Purchase Insurance

If keeping high-risk people out of the insurance pool doesn't solve the underlying problems affecting the market, then maybe requiring low-risk people to enter it can. This is the third option for the government to consider: an "individual mandate" to buy insurance.

For our four-person country, playing this scenario out is straightforward: the insurance company will charge everyone $9,200 for a policy, everyone will buy it, and the price will never change. Not only will the market avoid the downward spiral, but the hospital will never have to raise the price of surgery. These are the upsides. But of course, there are downsides: namely, Alonso and Beatriz are forced to buy something that costs more than it's worth to them. This may be especially frustrating to Alonso. Since he values insurance at $400 per year, the mandate effectively forces him to spend $8,800 more than he wants to.

From the perspective of the country as a whole, the individual mandate offers tremendous benefits. But to many of the individuals themselves, it comes at a great cost. They may be covered, but they're not necessarily happy.

...

While a hypothetical four-person country with one medical procedure is clearly unrealistic, the simplification allows us to explore the logic of how an insurance market works. At its heart (pardon the pun), an insurance market comes down to expected value: the probability of getting sick times the price of getting fixed. The more likely someone is to need care, the more insurance will be worth, and the more expensive it will be. Conversely, the more low-risk customers there are in the pool, the cheaper insurance will become. This logic doesn't just apply to an invented country. It applies to an actual one like the United States, too. For while the real-life details are different — a population of 330 million; a greater diversity of risk profiles; a higher number of maladies; and an insurance and hospital industry that expects to make a profit — the underlying structure is the same. Of course, as many experts point out, medical procedures tend to be more expensive in the United States than elsewhere; for instance, the typical price for an M.R.I. scan in the U.S. is more than $1,400, compared to $450 in Britain. Still, even if the cost of medical care came down, so would everyone's expected value for insurance, leaving the underlying logic of the market unchanged.

Without insurance, many people would not be able to afford the medical care they need. When we join together and pool our resources, though, we can receive care that we'd otherwise miss out on. This is why health insurance is so helpful: it allows us to pay together what we couldn't pay alone. But it's also why insurance can be so contentious. By its very nature, insurance can only function if some people put in more than they take out. There's no getting around this. For while buying insurance allows us to avoid one kind of risk — the risk of going bankrupt — it means accepting another kind: namely, the risk of buying something that you'll never actually use.

Discussion Questions:

- Which of the three policy options — allowing people to decide whether to buy insurance; allowing insurance companies to deny coverage to high-risk people; and requiring everyone to buy insurance — do you prefer and why?

- For the option that you chose, who might be some winners and losers? For individuals and institutions who think the policy makes them worse off, can you think of anything that would make their situations more palatable?

- Most developed nations provide health care coverage to all of their citizens. The United States does not; Medicaid only covers the poor, while Medicare only covers people who are 65 years and older. While some Americans believe the government should cover everyone, others are concerned that it would be too expensive. Which medical procedures do you think the government should cover (if any), and which do you think should require private insurance?

PART SIX

INSPIRING A SOCIETY OF REASON

'M writing to you in early 2021 from Adelaide, Australia, a garden-filled city on the continent's southern coast. I arrived in Australia in March of last year, just as the coronavirus began to sweep across the globe. Five days after I landed, the federal government sealed its border to foreigners, while state and local governments closed non-essential businesses, cancelled sports, and required contact tracing. As frustrating as the disruptions were, Australians went along with them, and life soon returned to normal. Within a few months, students were once again walking down the streets in backpacks. Restaurants were bustling. Other than the stickers on grocery store floors telling people where to stand and sign-in sheets on café tables, you wouldn't know that the coronavirus was still raging full-force in countries around the world...and nowhere more so than in the United States. In Australia, fewer than a thousand citizens have died from the virus *in total*. In the United States, more than twice that number died *yesterday*. Of course, this being a letter about math, I readily acknowledge that the U.S. is a larger country. We have roughly ten times as many people as does Australia...and almost 400 times as many COVID deaths. Americans represent 4% of the human population and roughly 20% of coronavirus cases. It is not, as any seventh grader can attest, *proportional*.

And yet as destructive as the virus has been, what's worse is the way that we as a country have responded to it. Instead of quantifying the tradeoffs between safeguarding public health and maintaining the economy, we argue over whether the virus is a hoax. Instead of evaluating strategies for slowing its spread, we argue about whether social distancing is a sign of tyranny. At the state capitol in Michigan, protesters surrounded legislators with machine guns to discourage them from enacting a quarantine. At the Sesame Place theme park in Pennsylvania, a couple broke an employee's jaw for asking them to wear masks. This isn't normal.

I've heard of nothing like this happening in Australia. When I asked a friend here why, I figured it might be due to the country's history. "Australia started out as a prison colony," I offered. "Do you think that's why you were so receptive to policies like the mask mandate?" She rolled her eyes. "We're wearing masks not because we're *obedient*. We're doing it because we're in a pandemic and because the policy makes sense." *Because the policy makes sense.* Here, citizens are grounding their behavior in reason. Back home, they're literally having fist fights on Sesame Street. It's heartbreaking.

Yet it isn't out of character. What I've observed over the past nine months from a hemisphere away (and what you've experienced firsthand) is similar to what I witnessed during the Affordable Care Act town hall meeting in Virginia twelve years ago: a frenzy of anger and a cacophony of name-calling; not just the breakdown of reason but the blatant mockery of it. At this point, it's hard to discern whether we actually disagree about issues like the individual mandate and the efficacy of masks, or whether we're simply using them as bells to signal the next round in an ongoing national cage fight.

The United States is the oldest continuous democracy on Earth, and mathematics is the most powerful prism for analysis that humans have ever devised. Just as Galileo helped to do four centuries ago, we as educators can be the ones to spark a renaissance in critical thinking. Cable news is unlikely to expose us to new ideas. Instead of expanding our understanding of the world, broadcasters like Fox News and MSNBC profit by narrowing it. Social media is unlikely to help, either; on Twitter, the phrase "on one hand, on the other" alone will cost you 10% of your allocated characters. No, if we're to kindle a nation of Citizens Math, it won't happen on a screen. It needs to start in the classroom.

Looking through Math-Colored Glasses

Pandemics are difficult; there are no easy answers for how to best reconcile individual liberty and social welfare. Like Australia, should the United States have grounded domestic air travel early in the outbreak? Just as the Australian state of New South Wales banned outdoor concerts, should the American state of

South Dakota have cancelled its 400,000-person Sturgis Motorcycle Rally? These are complicated issues. What's not complicated, though, is the mathematics beneath them.

When a virus spreads, it spreads *exponentially*. Instead of growing by a constant *number* of people, a virus grows by a constant *multiple*. Epidemiologists refer to this multiple as R-naught (R_0). In 2014, the Ebola virus that spread across parts of Africa had a R_0 value of approximately 2, which meant that on average an infected person would pass the virus to two new people, who would in turn pass it to two more, resulting in a doubling pattern of new cases: 2, 4, 8, 16, and so on. Because the coronavirus is transmitted more easily than Ebola is, because its symptoms take longer to appear, and because people infected with the coronavirus remain contagious for longer, it has a higher R_0 value. According to the Centers for Disease Control, the R_0 value for coronavirus is roughly 6. This is extremely dangerous. For while the number of new infections in a given town or city will appear small at first (6, 36, 216), the cases quickly explode: 1296, 7776, 46,656. Indeed, this is exactly what happened across the United States. When the virus first arrived in an area, people looked around and thought, "I don't personally know anyone infected with the coronavirus. The concerns are overblown." But within a month or two, hospitals were full, nurses were overwhelmed, and morgues were renting refrigeration trucks to store the excess corpses.

So should the American government have shut down domestic air travel? Should states have cancelled "super-spreader events" like rallies and festivals that help the local economy but accelerate the outbreak? It's hard to say. While Australia fared far better than did the United States, it's also an island where 60% of the population lives in four cities. It's possible that the policies that were so effective here in Australia would not have been feasible in a country as large as the United States. Still, though I'm uncertain about what the ideal response is, I am certain that any rigorous discussion of an outbreak must involve exponential growth...and that the discussion we've been having as Americans has not. We've argued a lot about whether conservatives are anti-science and liberals are anti-freedom. But we've reasoned much less about math. Instead of treating the pandemic as a partisan issue to fight over, imagine if we'd approached it as a problem to solve. Instead of arguing over "tyranny" and "conspiracies," imagine if we'd reasoned about R-naught values and ICU capacities. If you're a math educator, these are the conversations you get to facilitate. This is the citizenry you get to create. This is the country we need you to foster.

Of course, mathematics can help shed light on critical issues other than the virus. In the past five years, more than 5,000 people in the United States have been killed in violent encounters with the police. These include Tamir Rice in Cleveland, Freddie Gray in Baltimore, Atatiana Jefferson in Fort Worth, and Breonna Taylor in Louisville. Yet while smartphones and body cameras mean that more people finally agree that a problem exists, they disagree about how it's distributed and whom it affects. According to a 2020 Pew Research survey, 61% of Republicans assume that that police officers use the correct amount of force in each situation, compared to just 14% of Democrats. 64% of Republicans believe that police officers treat all races and ethnic groups the same, compared to 10% of Democrats. It's as though partisans are watching the same cell phone footage but from completely different realities.

Instead of viewing policing through a partisan lens, what happens when we view it through a mathematical one? In the wake of the 1991 beating of California motorist Rodney King, the Los Angeles Police Department released one of the few publicly available sources of data on excessive use of force. The report detailed how the roughly 24,000 complaints that the LAPD had received over the previous five-year period had been distributed among its 8,000 officers.

Officers by Number of Complaints Received (LAPD, 1986-1990)

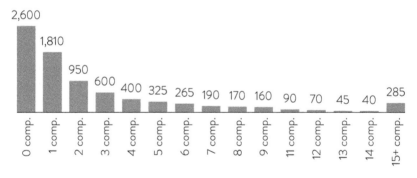

Between 1986 and 1990, 2600 officers — roughly a third of the LAPD — received no complaints, while another 1700 received one. At the other end of the spectrum, 285 officers received 15 or more complaints. While this worst-offending group only represented 4% of the police force, it accounted for 23% of all complaints. Ten percent of officers accounted for nearly half of the complaints.

Following the beating of Rodney King, Los Angelenos were rightfully angry, and many may have concluded that the LAPD needed to allocate resources to retrain every officer. Based on the data, though, a more targeted approach might have been more effective. Since police violence was distributed differently than how many assumed, addressing it might have required a different approach than what many proposed. (The concentration of bad behavior isn't unique to Los Angeles. In May 2020, Minneapolis resident George Floyd died after being suffocated by Derek Chauvin, an officer who over the course of his career had received eighteen complaints of excessive force. According to Minneapolis Chief of Police Medaria Arradondo, department leadership knew that Chauvin was an outlier and was not representative of the typical officer. However, the city's contract with the police union made it difficult to remove bad apples from the force.)

So what about the racial composition of victims of excessive force?

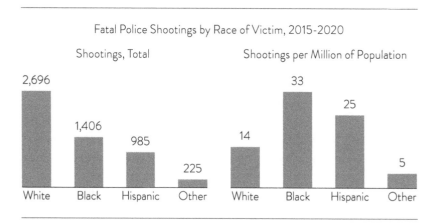

Fatal Police Shootings by Race of Victim, 2015-2020

Between 2015 and 2020, more white people were fatally shot by police officers than were Black or Hispanic people, but this is to be expected; they represent a much larger share of the country. When we account for population size, though, we find that even though more white people were killed in total, Black and Hispanic people were killed at a higher *rate*. For every million white people, 14 were killed, compared to per-million rates of 33 for Blacks and 25 for Hispanics. Contrary to what many people believe, according to the data a Black person in the United States is 2.4 times more likely to be fatally shot by a police officer than is a white person, while a Hispanic person is 1.8 times more likely. Once again, mathematics presents a very different picture than what millions of Americans assume.

Excessive use of force by police is a serious problem. If we're serious about addressing it, then we need to do more than scream at one another about it.

We need to analyze it. Math can help us do that.

Of course, there's a limit to what mathematics can do. When it comes to excessive force by police, there are many aspects of the issue that are not captured by the data, such as the emotional toll that mistrust has on officers and civilians and the alienation that arises from profiling and racial mistreatment. Even when mathematical models are relatively robust, they're only helpful if people use them in good faith; regardless of how unbiased numbers may be in and of themselves, there will always be people who misinterpret them, or manipulate them, or ignore them, or even invent their own. Mathematics cannot solve this problem. Nor can it resolve every issue. Take the death penalty. While some Americans believe it's immoral for the government to execute a prisoner convicted of murder, others believe in the doctrine of an eye for an eye. When it comes to debating *whether* the state should apply the death penalty, this is a fundamentally philosophical or spiritual question. Mathematics has little to offer.

But when it comes to illuminating *how* the state applies the penalty, math offers quite a lot. Between 1980 and 2007, courts in North Carolina convicted 14,500 people of murder and sentenced 328 to death. According to the data, the most important factor in determining whether a defendant received the death penalty was not the nature of the crime or even the race of the perpetrator (as many assume). It was the race of the victim. When the victim was white, the defendant was three times as likely to be sentenced to death as when the victim was Black. In the United States, partisans may disagree about the morality of executions, but we must still agree on their composition.

Just as words cannot fully capture the totality of reality, neither can math. Still, as limited as mathematics is, it's the most powerful tool that humans have invented for objectively analyzing the world around us. Quantitative reasoning may not be able to illuminate all of the challenges we face as a national community, but we're unlikely to solve any of them without it.

Separating Ego from Analysis

From what I've observed on social media and elsewhere, more and more Americans are personalizing information and positions that aren't personal. Some have conflated subjective experience and objective reality so completely, in fact, that it influences how they speak. "I *feel* like the coronavirus is going away," they declare, as though intuition is a substitute for evidence. When someone makes a statement that's factually inaccurate, for many the default reaction is not to critique the information but to criticize the person: "You're wrong." This over-personalization of the outside world is dangerous and stifles productive discourse. By pegging our identities to a predefined version of the world, we risk becoming overly defensive when someone offers an alternative perspective and treating as a threat someone who might otherwise be a collaborator. This is why mathematics is so helpful. As a prism for dispassionate analysis, math helps us detach who we are from what we see. While this separation can be uncomfortable at first, it can also be liberating.

I discovered this profoundly during a 2015 sabbatical in Greece. I had traveled to the island of Lesbos to volunteer with refugees arriving by raft from Turkey. Many were Syrians fleeing a civil war. Others were from Afghanistan, Pakistan, and elsewhere hoping to find work in Europe. Because the Syrians were war refugees, the European Union provided them with food, clothing, shelter and, most importantly, an expedited ferry trip and entry to the mainland. The economic migrants, on the other hand, were herded to a ramshackle camp in an olive grove just outside of the village of Moria where they waited — often for weeks — for the Greek authorities to process their paperwork. There were few blankets, little shelter from the elements, and just one latrine for thousands of men, women, and children. The gnarled branches of the olive trees were gone, having long since been turned into firewood. When it rained, human waste covered the walkways and cast a stench over the area.

I wasn't a lawyer, so I wasn't able to provide legal aid. Though I had volunteered as an EMT during graduate school, I lacked the skills and supplies to treat the diabetes, broken bones, and even stabbings that arose in the camp. So I considered how else I might help. By the time they arrived on the island, many of the migrants had been walking for months, and almost all of them had ragged beards. I decided to build an area on the edge of the camp where refugees could get a free shave. To construct the "Shave Shack," I enlisted the help of an Iranian migrant, Mehrdad. We used a discarded UN tarp as the roof, dug a fire pit to heat water, and nailed mirrors to the trunks of trees. One evening, while tidying up, I looked out over the camp, where hundreds of people were hunched over campfires warming their hands, exhausted and expressionless. As the light faded, I wondered to myself, "What should happen to this place?"

Immediately a voice inside of me answered. *The UN should build beds and bathrooms*, it said. *The EU should cook meals and provide coats. This camp is awful, and someone needs to improve it.* As soon as the voice finished, another countered. *Consider Mehrdad*, it instructed. *He's in his fifties. He only speaks a few words of English and probably knows no German. If he can't find a job in Tehran, what are his prospects in Berlin?* Almost all of the migrants in Moria were trying to reach places like Germany, Sweden, and Austria, countries that provided residents with generous services like free health care and social security. These social safety nets had already been strained by the economic downturn a few years earlier, and they risked crumbling under the weight of an influx of unemployed foreigners. Though improving the camp struck me as the humane thing to do, I understood why European governments were reluctant to do so. The more comfortable the camp became, the more migrants it would attract. The more migrants it attracted, the more European governments might have to spend on social services for them.

This interior tug-of-war surprised me. My family is from the Middle East. I like to think of myself as a generous person. If someone had asked me prior to arriving on Lesbos what should happen, I wouldn't have had to think: *Fix the camp.* But once I did arrive — once I did play out the situation logically — my confidence softened. My certainty wavered. In the end, the immediacy of the humanitarian argument won out in me. But I felt less dogmatic. I felt less sure. Most of all, I felt more peaceful, as though someone had released me from a straitjacket of ideological rigidity. Though I never affixed numbers to the crisis or wrote a lesson about it, the thought process in which I engaged on that hilltop was fundamentally mathematical. It was an analysis of tradeoffs, one which left me more open-minded than when I'd begun and which still feels epiphanic more than half a decade later. It wasn't simply that I understood the situation differently. It's that I realized in that moment *just how rare* feelings of ambivalence have become in our modern information era, and just how dangerous a media ecosystem is that reassures us that whatever we think, we're absolutely right. At this precarious moment in our nation's history, it's more important than ever that children develop an appreciation for informed ambivalence and a tolerance for opposing perspectives.

The math classroom is where we can do this. Instead of only prioritizing questions that converge on a single answer, math teachers can challenge students to consider ones that don't. *Should Major League Baseball standardize outfield dimensions? Should Americans be required to buy health insurance? Do bad days make good days feel better, and is there an upside to feeling sad?* None of these questions has a definitive answer, but all are explorable with math. I visited a classroom in Colorado once where students were debating the fairest way to pay for shoes. Upon learning that a pair of popular sneakers weighed nearly twice as much in size 16 as it did in size 4, they used unit rates to reason that people with small feet were paying twice as much per ounce. "Does that seem fair?" the teacher asked. "We pay by weight when we buy meat at the deli. Why not when we buy shoes at the shoe store?"

As an exemplar of quantitative reasoning, you can inspire a generation of mathematical citizens who understand that true wisdom isn't revealed in the answers we find but in the questions we ask. *Should people with small feet pay less for shoes?* There's no right answer to that, but the answer isn't what matters here. What matters is the permission we give ourselves to look at the world with fresh eyes and to consider how else it might work. Millions of Americans have become numb to conventional thinking and have wedded their identities to a singular orientation of reality. This limits us as a nation. It makes us fragile, defensive, antagonistic, and unaccommodatingly incurious. At its heart, mathematics is a tool for analyzing critically and imagining creatively. Ultimately, this may be the most valuable gift that you as a math educator can offer the country: an opportunity for students to wonder; the realization that an open mind may be the most patriotic mind of all.

Unlocking Our Full Potential

I believe that math class represents our best chance — and maybe our last hope — for improving the quality of American discourse and restoring a commitment to reason. My goal in writing you this letter has been to share a vision of what math class can be, and I hope you've found it helpful. Still, even if you share my enthusiasm for the power of mathematics and math teachers as incubators of a rational citizenry, there are a number of steps that we as a community will need to take before we can fulfill our full potential. Though we've explored these in depth already, it seems pedagogically fitting to recap them.

First, we must recognize what we mean when we refer to "mathematics" and acknowledge how rigid our approach to math instruction has remained for most of our history. For generations we've defined the purpose of math class as developing procedural fluency and conceptual understanding (including problem-solving strategies). Because these are the aspects that we've traditionally envisioned, the resources and strategies that we've prioritized are those that correspond to them.

As a result, when an innovation modernizes how we present math — skills practice on YouTube, for instance, or word problems filmed with a GoPro — we herald it as "revolutionary," even though it preserves the same fundamental learning experience that students have always received. This experience of learning math isn't bad. It's simply incomplete.

The second step that we need to take as educators, then, is to understand how our traditional approach to math instruction is lacking and incorporate activities that complete it. In particular, we must distinguish between mathematics as a subject to look at and mathematics as a lens to look with. In addition to activities that use an ostensibly "real world" scenario to illustrate some underlying mathematical procedure or concept, we must incorporate ones in which students *apply* those procedures and concepts to learn something new about the world. It isn't enough to use foul shots as a context for parabolas and milkshakes as a setup for linear equations. We must also provide students with opportunities to turn the telescope of mathematics around and train it on reality: to use parabolas to debate whether baseball stadiums should be standardized and linear functions to analyze the effects of speeding fines on low-income communities. By honoring the complete nature of mathematics, we will provide a more expansive and fulfilling experience of learning it.

Of course, it's one thing to *understand* what a complete math education entails. It's quite another to put it into practice. Even when we math educators recognize the importance of incorporating authentic real-world explorations into our classrooms, we offer a range of justifications for why we can't. These include the beliefs that teachers in other content areas are better positioned to facilitate conversations about social issues, that students must formally master mathematics before they can apply it, and that year-end tests limit what teachers can do rather than simply inform it. As widespread as these explanations are, they rest on flawed assumptions and can easily be overcome. If we're to achieve our full capacity as math educators, we must quiet the mindsets that have long stymied our profession and kept us from embracing how truly powerful we are.

Even if we commit ourselves to transforming our classrooms into forums for real-world discourse, though, it'll only matter if students continue to congregate in them for shared learning experiences. The final step we must take towards realizing a more expansive vision of math class is to resist efforts to replace teachers with algorithms and strand students in silos of individualized learning. Across the country, more and more schools (and even entire states) are adopting software to digitize math instruction. While "personalized learning" programs may have a helpful role to play within a broader instructional strategy, there are a number of forces at work which are hastening their proliferation, and possibly in dangerous ways. If we're not careful, technologies which were originally intended to address a narrow problem — bolstering gaps in fluency, for instance — could exceed our ability to constrain them and suffocate the spirit of public education. Learning is a social process. Personalized learning, on the other hand, is rooted in the ideology that the purpose of school is to serve the individual alone. Of all the trends in American education, there may be none more dangerous than the notion that learning is digitizable and that classrooms are societally optional.

Acknowledging the historical incompleteness of math instruction. Honoring the full nature of math. Overcoming the mental blocks which have limited our potential as educators. Preserving learning as a social endeavor. It's a lot. But if we as a community can commit ourselves to taking these steps, then we may one day find ourselves in exactly the reality that so many of us have dreamed about: one in which people think critically, wonder passionately, and coexist kindly. I realize how strange it sounds to attribute so much possibility to math class. But it's true. I've seen what's possible. I've witnessed how powerful you are.

Creating a Legacy

In his book *Between the World and Me*, the writer Ta-Nehisi Coates beautifully captures what it means to be an inquisitive citizen. "This is what the best of the old heads meant when they spoke of being politically conscious," he wrote. "As much a series of actions as a state of being, a constant questioning, questioning as ritual, questioning as exploration rather than the search for certainty."

Math teachers are fundamentally askers of questions. When you peel away all of the other contributions that we make — motivational speeches, emotional counseling — questions are what we offer. As a nation, we have constructed a massive edifice to support teachers in doing this. We've built 100,000 public schools. We've optimized the routes of 500,000 school buses. We've installed chalkboards and whiteboards and LCD projectors and have bought millions of dry erase markers. And we've done all of this for one reason: so that when the roughly 50 million American schoolchildren walk through our classroom doors, we can greet them with a question.

And yet what are the questions we greet them with?

What is the cube root of 27?
How long does it take to drink a milkshake?
How many meatballs fit in a pot?

We can do better than that. The old familiar questions serve a purpose, yes. But we can ask more. We can ask questions that challenge students to think about the world more deeply.

In sixth grade, students learn how to calculate percents. When we eat at a restaurant, it's common to leave a tip of 15% of the total bill. What this means is that instead of compensating servers based on how hard they work, we compensate them based on how expensive the menu is. *Is a percent the fairest way to calculate a tip? If not, what might be some other ways to pay servers?*

In seventh grade, students learn about rates and proportions. Distracted driving kills thousands of Americans each year. If it takes six seconds to respond to a text message, in that time a driver going 35 miles per hour will travel the length of a football field, while one driving twice as fast will travel twice as far. *So which is more dangerous — texting in a residential area or on the highway — and how can we convince drivers to put down their phones?*

In eighth grade, students learn how to write and solve equations. Each year scores of children lose their hair to leukemia and other conditions. The organization Locks of Love provides them wigs from donated hair. On average, human hair grows 0.5 inches per month, and a complete wig requires ten 10-inch donations. *How long would it take for a single person to donate an entire wig's worth of hair…and how could a student-organized hair drive expedite the process?*

In high school, students learn about exponential decay. According to neuroscientists, remembering is an act of re-creation; each time you have a memory of an event, you recreate it from scratch, thereby changing a bit. This implies that the more times you remember something, the less accurate the memory becomes. *If we assume that fidelity deteriorates by a constant percent, how many times can remember something before no longer trust it?*

The old questions that we've always asked in math class have an important role to play. But we can go farther. We can ask so much more. My motivation for writing you this letter is to inspire you to see math class as representing something bigger than we've historically envisioned; to view your classroom as more than a place for questions that are pedagogically helpful but ultimately forgettable, but also as a forum for questions that challenge students to think creatively about the world and to live more actively in it. This is what mathematics allows. And for those of us who teach it, this is the opportunity we have.

Again, though, I readily acknowledge that creating mathematical citizens is not something that teachers are required to do. Reconsidering conventions in tipping and debating the consequences of a fallible memory do not appear in any state standards. In fact, the learning outcomes that states require and the results that districts measure may actually make it easier to justify doing less than to aspire to offer more. It's quite a pickle. If you've read this far, I assume it's because you're hungry to go beyond what's strictly necessary and are eager to help students apply mathematics to world's most important and interesting questions. And yet you operate within a system that doesn't demand them, may not see them, and sometimes even discourages them. So what to do?

In moments like this, I often turn to an essay penned by the astronomer Carl Sagan more than forty years ago. In 1977, NASA launched the Voyager 1 spacecraft towards the outer limits of our solar system. 3.7 billion miles later, Sagan asked engineers to turn the probe around and take a photo of the Earth before it faded into darkness. When the image was revealed, he mused about the portrait of our distant 'pale blue dot:'

> "The Earth is a very small stage in a vast cosmic arena. On it everyone you love, everyone you know, everyone you ever heard of, every human being who ever was, lived out their lives...Every hunter and forager, every hero and coward...every king and peasant...every mother and father, hopeful child...every teacher of morals, every corrupt politician...every saint and sinner in the history of our species lived there: on a mote of dust suspended in a sunbeam."

In moments when I feel torn between obligation and calling, I find strength in remembering that all of the problems that unsettle me and all of the dilemmas I face are temporary. They will expire, and soon. And so will I. Like our planet in the photo, I am but a flicker in the vast passage of time. Yet while some might interpret our cosmic irrelevance as an excuse to do nothing, I see it as permission to do anything. If I'm only here for a short time, after all, why not make the most of it...even if the most of it isn't strictly required?

If you're reading this, there's a good chance that you're a math educator. Maybe you've been in the classroom for decades or maybe you've just begun. But wherever you are in your journey, one day that journey will end. One day you'll erase the board for the final time and take one last look at your classroom. When you do, what do you want to have happened there? What conversations do you want to have led? What insights do you hope to have sparked? One day you'll teach your last lesson. (One day I'll write mine.) Like NASA's Voyager spacecraft, all of us will at some point or another reflect back on the time we spent in education. When we arrive to that distant tomorrow and step out into the world, how might the world spin better thanks to the decisions we make today?

By the time you read this, the worst of the coronavirus pandemic may have passed. The vaccines will have been injected. The lockdowns will have eased, and a sense of normalcy may have begun to return. Even once we're free of this particular virus, though, a deeper infirmity will remain: the irrationality that infects our body politic and undermines our ability to function as a nation. It's tempting to blame our chaotic national response to COVID-19 on politicians and media personalities, but the fact is that they're a reflection of us. The reason we responded so counterproductively to the coronavirus is the same reason we reacted so acerbically to health care reform: because we've exorcised logic from our discourse and have come to tolerate an absence of rigor in our own thinking. If we continue to do this, it isn't just Americans who will perish. America might, too.

As math educators, we are uniquely positioned to restore a commitment to reason. Indeed, we may have more influence over the trajectory of our democracy than anyone else in the country. For while Carl Sagan could only reflect on the past, we get to write the future. Every future president. Every Supreme Court justice. Every small town mayor, bus driver, and Little League Coach. Everyone who will determine the future of our country is seated in a classroom today. If the country of tomorrow is to function more effectively than the one we occupy today, we'll need to get better at thinking rigorously and engaging with one another more respectfully about the challenges we share, from climate change to the acceleration of technology, the psychology of consumerism to the individual mandate.

Almost every issue we encounter in our lives can be better understood through the prism of math. The math classroom is the perfect place to discuss them. So let's embrace the opportunity we have. Let's reimagine what's possible in math class. Let's fulfill our potential as educators so that, when we do close the classroom door and step out of the school building for the final time, you might emerge into a world illuminated by reason and vibrating with mutual respect. A reality that we'll be proud to have shaped. A nation of rigorous thinkers. A community of Citizens Math.

I hope you've found this letter helpful. Wherever it may find you, I hope it finds you well.

Yours,
Karim

ENDNOTES

Part One: Math Class in the Age of Certainty

In Tampa, opponents of the bill shut the discussion down by banging on doors and chanting "tyranny!" "Town Hall Meeting on Health Care Turns Ugly," *CNN*, August 7, 2009, https://www.cnn.com/2009/POLITICS/08/07/ health.care.scuffles/index.html.

On Long Island, police had to escort a congressman to his car... Alex Isenstadt, "Town Halls Gone Wild," *Politico*, July 31, 2009, https://www. politico.com/story/2009/07/town-halls-gone-wild-025646.

Protestors in Texas waved signs depicting President Obama with a Hitler mustache... Jim Spellman, "Tea Party Movement Has Anger, No Dominant Leaders," *CNN*, September 12, 2009, https://edition.cnn.com/2009/ POLITICS/09/12/tea.party.express/index.html.

...while those in Maryland hanged a congressman in effigy. Glenn Thrush, "Rep. Kratovil Hung in Effigy by Health Care Protester," *On Congress Blog*, July 28, 2009, https://www.politico.com/blogs/on-congress/2009/07/ rep-kratovil-hung-in-effigy-by-health-care-protester-update-020260.

...newspaper headlines describing "Health Debate Turns Hostile"... Ian Urbina, "Beyond Beltway, Health Debate Turns Hostile," *New York Times*, August 7, 2009, https://www.nytimes.com/2009/08/08/us/ politics/08townhall.html.

... a local rabbi rose to offer an opening prayer. "Representative James Moran Town Hall Meeting," filmed August 25, 2009, https://www.c-span.org/ video/?288530-1/representative-james-moran-town-hall-meeting.

...tens of thousands of people die each year due to inadequate access to medical care. David Cecere, "New Study Finds 45,000 Deaths Annually Linked to Lack of Health Coverage," *The Harvard Gazette*, September 17, 2009, https://news.harvard.edu/gazette/story/2009/09/new-study-finds-45000-deaths-annually-linked-to-lack-of-health-coverage/.

...a majority of Americans agreed that insurance companies should not be allowed to deny coverage based on pre-existing conditions. S. Ward Casscells, et al., "Americans on Health Care Reform: Results from Polls Conducted with Zogby International, Inc.," *Transactions of the American Clinical and Climatological Association* 121 (2010), 267-280, https://www.ncbi.nlm.nih.gov/pmc/articles/PMC2917127//.

Today, 85% of American adults think our discourse has become more negative in recent years... Bruce Drake and Jocelyn Kiley, "Americans Say the Nation's Political Debate Has Grown More Toxic and 'Heated' Rhetoric Could Lead to Violence," *Pew Research Center Fact Tank*, July 18, 2019, https://www.pewresearch.org/fact-tank/2019/07/18/americans-say-the-nations-political-debate-has-grown-more-toxic-and-heated-rhetoric-could-lead-to-violence.

...a 2019 analysis of the right-leaning Fox News found that 86% of its segments... Allison Fisher, "FOXIC: Fox News Network's Dangerous Climate Denial 2019," *Public Citizen*, August 13, 2019, https://mkus3lurbh3lbztg254fzode-wpengine.netdna-ssl.com/wp-content/uploads/public-citizen-fox-new-climate-denial-report-2019.pdf.

...more than twice as many Republicans as Democrats think that policies aimed at reducing the effects of climate change do more harm than good. *Pew Research Center Fact Tank*, https://www.pewresearch.org/fact-tank/2020/04/21/how-americans-see-climate-change-and-the-environment-in-7-charts/ft_2020-04-21_earthday_05/

...two-thirds of viewers of MSNBC viewers thought the virus came about naturally... *Pew Research Center's American News Pathways* data tool, https://www.pewresearch.org/pathways-2020/covidcreate/main_source_of_election_news/us_adults/.

29% of Fox News viewers believed that a vaccine would be available within a year of the outbreak... *Pew Research Center's American News Pathways* data tool, https://www.pewresearch.org/pathways-2020/covidvacc/main_source_of_election_news/us_adults/.

In 2019 alone, Fox News and MSNBC combined for nearly $2 billion worth of ad sales... Michael Kassel, "Election Boom: Here's How Much Money CNN, Fox News And MSNBC Are Expected to Make in 2020," *Mediaite*, January 8, 2020, https://www.mediaite.com/tv/election-boom-heres-how-much-ad-money-cnn-fox-news-and-msnbc-are-expected-to-make-in-2020/.

...Americans are more divided now than at any time in the past quarter century. Pew Research Center, "The Partisan Divide on Political Values Grows Even Wider," October 5, 2017, https://www.pewresearch.org/politics/2017/10/05/the-partisan-divide-on-political-values-grows-even-wider/.

...a quarter of Republicans today say they'd never date a liberal... Anna Brown, "Most Democrats Who Are Looking for a Relationship Would Not Consider Dating a Trump Voter," *Pew Research Center Fact Tank*, April 24, 2020, https://www.pewresearch.org/fact-tank/2020/04/24/most-democrats-who-are-looking-for-a-relationship-would-not-consider-dating-a-trump-voter/.

...algorithms provide users their own tailor-made streams of posts designed to be — in the words of a company spokesperson — useful and relevant. Caitlin Dewey, "98 Personal Data Points that Facebook Uses to Target Ads to You," *Washington Post*, August 19, 2016, https://www.washingtonpost.com/news/the-intersect/wp/2016/08/19/98-personal-data-points-that-facebook-uses-to-target-ads-to-you/.

...a group of employees warned about the dangers of the system they'd built. Jeff Horwitz and Deepa Seetharaman, "Facebook Executives Shut Down Efforts to Make the Site Less Divisive," *Wall Street Journal*, May 26, 2020, https://www.wsj.com/articles/facebook-knows-it-encourages-division-top-executives-nixed-solutions-11590507499.

More than half of American adults today get their news from Facebook…
Elisa Shearer and Elizabeth Grieco, "Americans Are Wary of the Role Social
Media Sites Play in Delivering the News," Pew Research Center, October 2,
2019, https://www.journalism.org/2019/10/02/americans-are-wary-of-the-
role-social-media-sites-play-in-delivering-the-news/, cited in Samantha
Power, "Two Things Facebook Still Needs to Do to Reduce the Spread of
Misinformation," *Washington Post*, October 23, 2020, https://www.
washingtonpost.com/opinions/samantha-power-facebook-reduce-spread-
misinformation/2020/10/23/d54c1bda-1496-11eb-bc10-40b25382f1be_
story.html.

**Since 1920, Republicans and Democrats have cast nearly 2 billion votes for
president, and in that entire time Republicans are ahead by just 0.3%.** *Dave
Leip's Atlas of U.S. Presidential Elections*, https://uselectionatlas.org/
RESULTS/, accessed January 7, 2021.

Mathematical Vignette: Fake Discounts

Citizen Math Lesson. "Coupon Clipping," *Citizen Math*, https://www.
citizenmath.com/lessons/coupon-clipping, accessed January 11, 2021.

**Under Fair and Square, the average list price of an item at JCPenney was
40% lower than before.** Alexander Chernev, "Can There Ever Be a Fair
Price? Why Jcpenney's Strategy Backfired," *Harvard Business Review*, May
29, 2012, https://hbr.org/2012/05/can-there-ever-be-a-fair-price.

Within a year of the transition, sales at some stores fell by 30%. Kelsey
Lindsey, "Was Ron Johnson right?" *RetailDive*, March 1, 2016, https://www.
retaildive.com/news/was-ron-johnson-right/414481/.

**While visiting a mall in Cincinnati, a mother explained her decision to
abandon JCPenney.** WCPO9, "JC Penney Pricing Strategy Comes Under
Fire," *YouTube*, May 16, 2013, https://youtu.be/S-_A6sW3IPE

Under California law, retailers who describe an item as being "on sale"…
Davis & Gilbert LLP, "California Alleges Four of the Largest U.S. Retailers
Engage in 'False Reference Pricing,'" press release, January 30, 2017, https://
www.dglaw.com/press-alert-details.cfm?id=701.

In 2016, the attorney for the city of Los Angeles sued JCPenney, Kohl's, Sears, and Macy's for deceptive pricing. Los Angeles City Attorney's Office, "Los Angeles City Attorney Mike Feuer Sues Four Major National Retailers, Alleging False Reference Pricing," press release, December 8, 2016, https://www.lacityattorney.org/post/2016/12/08/los-angeles-city-attorney-mike-feuer-sues-four-major-national-retailers-alleging-false-re.

Part Two: The New Old Things

...44% of middle school students said they'd rather take out the garbage than do their math homework. Research Now, "Math Relevance to U.S. Middle School Students: A Survey Commissioned by Raytheon Company," February 2012, https://www.raytheon.com/sites/default/files/news/rtnwcm/groups/corporate/documents/content/rtn12_studentsmth_results.pdf.

In the first half of the 1900s, most American math textbooks emphasized mechanical drill. D. Baker et al., "One Hundred Years of Elementary School Mathematics in the United States: A Content Analysis and Cognitive Assessment of Textbooks from 1900 to 2000," *Journal for Research in Mathematics Education* 41 (2010), 383-423, https://doi.org/10.5951/JRESEMATHEDUC.41.4.0383.

By 2009, his eponymous Khan Academy was attracting more than 200,000 visitors each month. Ashish Kumar Sen, "Bookmark: The Prof Who Keeps His Shirt On," *Outlook*, June 28, 2010, https://magazine.outlookindia.com/story/bookmark-the-prof-who-keeps-his-shirt-on/265875.

A Houston Public Media story heard on NPR suggested how Khan was "revolutionizing online education." Abner Fletcher, "How Tutoring His Cousin Led Sal Khan to Revolutionize Online Education," *Houston Matters*, March 7, 2019, https://www.houstonpublicmedia.org/articles/news/2019/03/07/324483/how-tutoring-his-cousin-led-sal-khan-to-a-career-in-education/.

An article in Forbes described how Khan Academy was "blowing up traditional models" of school... Stephen J. Meyer, "Salman Khan: The World's Best-Known Teacher is Learning to Lead," *Forbes*, Dec. 3, 2014, https://www.forbes.com/sites/stevemeyer/2014/12/03/salman-khan-the-worlds-best-known-teacher-is-learning-to-lead/?sh=6761069060d4.

TIME named Sal one of its 100 most influential people on the planet... Bill Gates, "TIME 100: The List: Salman Khan," *TIME*, April 18, 2012, http://content.time.com/time/specials/packages/article/0,28804,2111975_2111976_2111942,00.html.

...Businessweek went so far as to anoint him the "Messiah of Math." Bryant Urstadt, "Salman Khan: The Messiah of Math," *Bloomberg Businessweek*, May 19, 2011, https://www.bloomberg.com/news/articles/2011-05-19/salman-khan-the-messiah-of-math.

The state of Idaho even launched a pilot to incorporate the resource statewide. Adam Cotterell, "48 Idaho Schools 'Flip The Classroom' And Pilot Khan Academy Online Learning," *Boise State Public Radio*, September 3, 2013, https://www.boisestatepublicradio.org/post/48-idaho-schools-flip-classroom-and-pilot-khan-academy-online-learning#stream/0.

"So to get the 20 out of the way from the left-hand side..." Salman Khan, "Equations with variables on both sides, 20 − 7x = 6x − 6," *Khan Academy*, https://www.khanacademy.org/math/algebra/x2f8bb11595b61c86:solve-equations-inequalities/x2f8bb11595b61c86:linear-equations-variables-both-sides/v/solving-equations-2, transcribed by the author.

In a 2011 interview, Khan described the process he uses when preparing his lessons. Clive Thompson, "How Khan Academy Is Changing the Rules of Education," *Wired*, July 15, 2011, https://www.wired.com/2011/07/ff-khan/.

In fact, it awarded Illustrative Math's middle school curriculum the highest possible score in every evaluation category. "LearnZillion Illustrative Mathematics 6-8 Math (2019)," *EdReports Report Center*, https://www.edreports.org/reports/overview/learnzillion-illustrative-mathematics-6-8-math-2019.

The cost of a babysitting service on a cruise is $10 for the first hour and $12 for each additional hour. EngageNY, "Lesson 17: Comparing Tape Diagram Solutions to Algebraic Solutions," *EngageNY NYS Common Core Mathematics Curriculum Grade 7*, n.d., https://www.engageny.org/resource/grade-7-mathematics-module-2-topic-c-lesson-17/file/60071, accessed January 7, 2021.

Kiran is trying to save $144 to buy a new guitar. Illustrative Mathematics, "Lesson 4: Reasoning about Equations and Tape Diagrams (Part 1)," *Illustrative Mathematics Grade 7*, 2017-2019, https://curriculum.illustrativemathematics.org/MS/students/2/6/4/index.html, accessed January 7, 2021.

An equipment rental company charges a different late fee each day. EngageNY, "Lesson 5: The Power of Exponential Growth," *EngageNY NYS Common Core Mathematics Curriculum Algebra 1*, n.d., https://www.engageny.org/resource/algebra-i-module-3-topic-lesson-5/file/52561, accessed January 7, 2021.

A purse contains 1 penny today. Illustrative Mathematics, "Lesson 1: Growing and Growing," *Illustrative Mathematics Algebra 1*, 2019, https://curriculum.illustrativemathematics.org/HS/teachers/1/5/1/index.html, accessed January 7, 2021.

A chessboard has 1 grain of wheat on the first square. Clifford A. Pickover, *The Math Book: From Pythagoras to the 57th Dimension* (New York: Sterling, 2009), cited in "Wheat and Chessboard Problem," *Wikipedia*, last updated December 23, 2020, https://en.wikipedia.org/wiki/Wheat_and_chessboard_problem, accessed January 7, 2021.

In a 2010 TED talk entitled "Math Class Needs a Makeover"... Dan Meyer, "Math Class Needs a Makeover," *TEDxNYED*, March 2010, video, https://www.ted.com/talks/dan_meyer_math_class_needs_a_makeover?language=en.

...a video of himself standing in the backyard filling a tank with a hose. Dan Meyer, "Water Tank," http://threeacts.mrmeyer.com/watertank/, accessed January 7, 2021.

The New Republic described Meyer as the "most famous math educator in America"… Boyce Upholt, "The Man Who Will Save Math," *New Republic*, December 1, 2015, https://newrepublic.com/article/124750/man-will-save-math.

Mathematical Vignette: Income, Rent, and Homelessness

Citizen Math Lesson. "Seeking Shelter," *Citizen Math*, https://www.citizenmath.com/lessons/seeking-shelter, accessed January 11, 2021.

While most of the proposals focused on practical matters like infrastructure and tax incentives, others bordered on shameless flattery. Shannon Liao, "The Eight Most Outrageous Things Cities Did to Lure Amazon for HQ2," *The Verge*, October 19, 2017, https://www.theverge.com/2017/10/19/16504042/amazon-hq2-second-headquarters-most-funny-crazy-pitches-proposals-stonecrest-new-york.

Amazon is one of the most successful companies in the world, and its new headquarters promised 50,000 new jobs. Cameron Sperance, "Amazon HQ2 Promotes 50,000 High-Paying Jobs (And A Shock To Your Housing Market)," *Forbes*, October 20, 2017, https://www.forbes.com/sites/bisnow/2017/10/20/amazon-hq2-promotes-50000-high-paying-jobs-and-a-shock-to-your-housing-market/?sh=62550560599b.

Many of these would pay more than $100,000 per year, nearly three times America's median annual income. Federal Reserve Bank of St. Louis, "Real Median Personal Income in the United States," https://fred.stlouisfed.org/series/MEPAINUSA672N, accessed January 11, 2021.

Median household income data for Seattle. United States Census Bureau American Community Survey cited in *Department of Numbers*, "Historical Inflation Adjusted Median Household Income for Seattle," https://www.deptofnumbers.com/income/washington/seattle/#household.

Median annual rent data for Seattle. United States Census Bureau American Community Survey cited in *Department of Numbers*, "Real Gross Rent History for Seattle," https://www.deptofnumbers.com/rent/washington/seattle/.

Point-in-time homelessness data for Seattle. Department of Housing and Urban Development, "2019 Point in Time Estimates of Homelessness," https://www.hud.gov/2019-point-in-time-estimates-of-homelessness-in-US, accessed January 8, 2021.

These [incentives] can include relocation payments and even a free bike. Alyson Krueger, "Want to Move to Our Town? Here's a $10,000 bonus and a free bike," *New York Times*, April 30, 2021, https://www.nytimes.com/2021/04/30/realestate/bentonville-arkansas-moving-incentive.html.

Part Three: Math As a Telescope

A science class designed a ball launcher... EngageNY, "Lesson 9: Graphing Quadratic Functions from Factored Form f(x) = a(x – m)(x – n)." *EngageNY NYS Common Core Mathematics Curriculum Algebra 1*, n.d., https://www.engageny.org/resource/algebra-i-module-4-topic-lesson-9/file/54016, accessed January 7, 2021.

Images of basketball shot. "Will It Hit the Hoop?" *Desmos*, https://teacher.desmos.com/activitybuilder/custom/56e0b6af0133822106a0bed1, accessed January 7, 2021.

Graph of Trajectory of Average MLB Home Run vs. Outfield Walls. "Out of Left Field," *Citizen Math*, https://www.citizenmath.com/lessons/out-of-left-field, accessed January 8, 2021.

Earlier this year I saw a headline in the education section of the New York Times... Patrick Honner, "Dangerous Numbers? Teaching About Data and Statistics Using the Coronavirus Outbreak," *New York Times*, February 27, 2020, https://www.nytimes.com/2020/02/27/learning/dangerous-numbers-teaching-about-data-and-statistics-using-the-coronavirus-outbreak.html.

Lin and Diego are drinking milkshakes... Illustrative Mathematics, "Lesson 12: Systems of Equations," *Illustrative Mathematics Grade 8*, 2017-2019, https://curriculum.illustrativemathematics.org/MS/teachers/3/4/12/index.html, accessed January 7, 2021.

And yet that did not stop EdReports from giving the curriculum a perfect score... "LearnZillion Illustrative Mathematics 6-8 Math (2019)," *EdReports Report Center*, https://www.edreports.org/reports/overview/learnzillion-illustrative-mathematics-6-8-math-2019.

Graphs of Speeding Fines and Savings, Bo and Ali. "You're So Fined," *Citizen Math*, https://www.citizenmath.com/lessons/you-re-so-fined, accessed January 8, 2021.

"Local authorities consistently approached law enforcement not as a means for protecting public safety," Holder explained... Adam B. Lerner, "Holder Slams Ferguson Police Force: 'Collection Agency'," *Politico*, March 4, 2014, https://www.politico.com/story/2015/03/eric-holder-slams-ferguson-police-force-collection-agency-115772.

"I have spent most of the last three weeks feeling as though I am failing miserably..." Brooke Powers, "Teacher Burn Out," *Powersfulmath*, January 19, 2017, https://powersfulmath.wordpress.com/2017/01/19/teacher-burn-out/.

Mathematical Vignette: Overselling Flights

Citizen Math Lesson. "Bumpy Flight," *Citizen Math*, https://www.citizenmath.com/lessons/bumpy-flight, accessed January 11, 2021.

On April 9, 2017, United Airlines made headlines... Lindsey Bever, "Doctor Who Was Dragged, Screaming, from United Airlines Flight Finally Breaks Silence," *Washington Post*, April 9, 2019, https://www.washingtonpost.com/transportation/2019/04/09/doctor-who-was-dragged-screaming-united-airlines-flight-finally-breaks-silence/.

Depending on the route and time of year, anywhere from 5 to 15 percent of passengers might miss a given flight... Haje Jan Kamps, "Why Do Airlines Overbook Their Flights?" *Tech Crunch*, April 11, 2017, https://techcrunch.com/2017/04/11/overbooking/.

In the United States, passengers who are involuntarily removed from a flight due to overbooking are legally entitled to compensation… United States Department of Transportation, "Bumping & Oversales," https://www. transportation.gov/individuals/aviation-consumer-protection/bumping-oversales, accessed January 11, 2021.

Delta dramatically increased the compensation its agents could offer… Richard Gonzales, "United Airlines Changes Its Policy on Displacing Customers," *The Two-Way*, April 14, 2017, https://www.npr.org/sections/ thetwo-way/2017/04/14/524033117/united-airlines-changes-its-policy-on-displacing-customers.

American promised that once passengers had boarded a plane, they would not be asked to move. *Associated Press*, "Overbooked Flight on Delta? You Now Could Get Nearly $10,000 to Give Up Your Seat," *Los Angeles Times*, April 14, 2017, https://www.latimes.com/business/la-fi-delta-overbooking-20170414-story.html.

Southwest did away with overbooking altogether. Julia Horowitz, "Southwest Airlines: We Won't Overbook Anymore," *CNN Business*, April 28, 2017, https://money.cnn.com/2017/04/27/news/companies/southwest-airlines-overbooking/.

Every day there are more than 45,000 flights in and out of the United States. United States Department of Transportation, "Air Traffic By The Numbers," last updated September 21, 2020, https://www.faa.gov/air_traffic/ by_the_numbers/.

Part Four: Addressing Common Concerns

The author explained how Mrs. Strole incorporated authentic real-world activities into her classroom… Stephen Sawchuk, "Math: The Most Powerful Civics Lesson You're Never Had," *EducationWeek*, November 26, 2019, https://www.edweek.org/teaching-learning/math-the-most-powerful-civics-lesson-youve-never-had/2019/11.

In 2019 more than 50,000 Americans died from overdosing on drugs such as OxyContin and heroin. Centers for Disease Control, National Center for Health Statistics, July 15, 2020, https://www.cdc.gov/nchs/nvss/vsrr/drug-overdose-data.htm.

Graphs of Pain Relief from Single Dose and Doses Needed for Full Relief. "House of Pain," *Citizen Math*, https://www.citizenmath.com/lessons/house-of-pain, accessed January 8, 2021.

Others turn to more potent opioids like fentanyl, a narcotic that's so powerful that just a few granules can prove fatal. Artemis Moshtaghian, "Police Officer Overdoses After Brushing Fentanyl Powder Off His Uniform," *CNN*, May 16, 2017, https://edition.cnn.com/2017/05/16/health/police-fentanyl-overdose-trnd/index.html.

"I don't think it's my job to tell them how to think or feel..." Alison Strole, quoted in Stephen Sawchuk, "Math: The Most Powerful Civics Lesson You're Never Had," *EducationWeek*, November 26, 2019, https://www.edweek.org/teaching-learning/math-the-most-powerful-civics-lesson-youve-never-had/2019/11.

Milestones in Warfare diagram. "About Time," *Citizen Math*, hhttps://www.citizenmath.com/lessons/about-time, accessed January 8, 2021.

An airplane flies at an altitude of 25,000 feet... EngageNY, "Lesson 5: Understanding Subtraction of Integers and Other Rational Numbers," *EngageNY NYS Common Core Mathematics Curriculum Grade 7*, n.d., https://www.engageny.org/resource/grade-7-mathematics-module-2-topic-lesson-5/file/59736, accessed January 7, 2021.

Plant A starts at 6 ft tall and grows at a constant rate... Illustrative Mathematics, "Lesson 12: Systems of Equations," *Illustrative Mathematics Grade 8*, 2017-2019, https://curriculum.illustrativemathematics.org/MS/teachers/3/4/12/index.html, accessed January 7, 2021.

...according to some experts, the most powerful motivator is intellectual need... Harel Guershon, "Intellectual Need," in *Vital Directions for Mathematics Education Research*, ed. Keith Leatham (New York: Springer, 2013), 119-151.

NY Regents Algebra 1 questions. The University of the State of New York, "Regents High School Examination: Algebra 1," January 22, 2020, https://www.nysedregents.org/algebraone/120/algone12020-exam.pdf.

The study found that teachers who incorporated just two real-world lessons into their curriculum... Kirabo Jackson and Alexey Makarin, "Can Online Off-the-Shelf Lessons Improve Student Outcomes? Evidence from a Field Experiment," *American Economic Journal: Economic Policy* 10, no. 3 (August 2018), 226-254, https://www.aeaweb.org/articles?id=10.1257/pol.20170211.

Mathematical Vignette: Rating Our Emotions

Citizen Math Lesson. "Downside Up," *Citizen Math*, https://www.citizenmath.com/lessons/downside-up, accessed January 11, 2021.

Part Five: Preserving the Social Purpose of School

The goal of the system, a school administrator explained... Preston Smith, quoted in Anya Kamenetz, "High Test Scores At A Nationally Lauded Charter Network, But At What Cost?" *NPR*, June 24, 2016, https://www.npr.org/sections/ed/2016/06/24/477345746/high-test-scores-at-a-nationally-lauded-charter-network-but-at-what-cost.

... a former supervisor at Alma Academy in San Jose described how he'd been left in charge of 90 students... Wesley Borja, quoted in Anya Kamenetz, "High Test Scores At A Nationally Lauded Charter Network, But At What Cost?" *NPR*, June 24, 2016, https://www.npr.org/sections/ed/2016/06/24/477345746/high-test-scores-at-a-nationally-lauded-charter-network-but-at-what-cost.

In a 2014 letter to the Santa Clara County school board... Lily Casillas, letter to Santa Clara County Board Members, June 16, 2014, https://www.sccoe.org/countyboard/Documents/2014-15/071614/8Correspondence.pdf, 28-29.

...among teachers whose schools used personalized learning, 17 percent devoted at least a quarter of their class time to working with students one-on-one... John F. Pane, "Informing Progress: Insights on Personalized Learning Implementation and Effects," Rand Corporation, 2017, https://www. rand.org/pubs/research_reports/RR2042.html.

In Georgia, only 7 percent of elementary teachers said that they felt comfortable with their new standards' emphasis on conceptual understanding... Susan Lee Swars and Cliff Chestnutt, "Transitioning to the Common Core State Standards for Mathematics: A Mixed Methods Study of Elementary Teachers' Experiences and Perspectives," *School Science and Mathematics* 116, no. 4 (April 2016), 212-224, https://doi.org/10.1111/ ssm.12171.

In 2013, the Los Angeles Unified School District launched a $1.3 billion initiative... Issie Lapowsky, "What Schools Must Learn From LA's iPad Debacle," *Wired*, May 8, 2015, https://www.wired.com/2015/05/los-angeles-edtech/.

...the median-sized school district consists of six schools and 15,000 students. United States Department of Education, National Center for Education Statistics, "Characteristics of the 100 Largest Public and Elementary School Districts in the United States: 1999-2000," https://nces. ed.gov/pubs2001/100_largest/discussion.asp

...an advanced program like DreamBox...can cost upwards of $7,000 per school. United States Department of Education Institute of Education Sciences, "DreamBox Learning," *What Works Clearinghouse*, December 2013, https://ies.ed.gov/ncee/wwc/Docs/InterventionReports/wwc_ dreambox_121013.pdf.

In Rhode Island, the state board of education's strategic plan... Rhode Island Council on Elementary and Secondary Education, *2020 Vision for Education: Rhode Island's Strategic Plan for PK–12 and Adult Education: 2015–2020*, August 24, 2015, https://www.ride.ri.gov/Portals/0/Uploads/Documents/ Board-of-Education/Strategic-Plan/RIStrategicPlanForPK20Education.pdf.

In Utah, "new school system models for personalized learning implementation." Utah State Board of Education, "Strategic Direction," September 2019, https://www.schools.utah.gov/file/174006b1-6ad5-44f2-8e1d-81079c6df543.

In Mississippi, "innovative programs to improve student outcomes, [including] online and personalized learning." Mississippi Board of Education, "Mississippi Board of Education Strategic Plan," last updated November 8, 2019, https://www.mdek12.org/MBE/StrategicPlan.

...school superintendents from 62 cities wrote a letter to Congress describing the dire financial situation they faced. Valerie Strauss, "K-12 School Leaders Warn of 'Disaster' from Huge Coronavirus-Related Budget Cuts as Layoffs and Furloughs Begin," *Washington Post*, May 8, 2020, https://www.washingtonpost.com/education/2020/05/08/k-12-school-leaders-warn-disaster-huge-coronavirus-related-budget-cuts-layoffs-furloughs-begin/.

In 2014, a consortium of philanthropies awarded $450,000 to a middle school in Alabama... Getting Smart Staff, "NGLC Makes 8 Launch and 30 Planning Grants for Next-Gen High Schools," *Getting Smart*, July 15, 2013, https://www.gettingsmart.com/2013/07/nglc-makes-8-launch-and-30-planning-grants-for-next-gen-high-schools/.

A year later, it provided $300,000 to schools in New Orleans... Josh McCarty, "New Schools for New Orleans and Educate Now! Awarding $1.5M in Grants to Support Personalized Learning Programs in New Orleans Schools," press release, April 21, 2015, http://www.newschoolsfneworleans.org/wp-content/uploads/2015/06/NSNO-and-Educate-Now-Awarding-1.5-in-Grants-to-Support-Personalized-Learning-Programs-in-New-Orleans-Schools-.pdf.

In 2018, Chicago Public Schools received a whopping $14 million to install personalized learning technology... LEAP Innovations, "Chicago Public Schools and LEAP Innovations Receive $14 Million in Grants from Chan Zuckerberg Initiative to Support School-Led Personalized Learning Programs," press release, May 1, 2018, https://www.prnewswire.com/news-releases/chicago-public-schools-and-leap-innovations-receive-14-million-in-grants-from-chan-zuckerberg-initiative-to-support-school-led-personalized-learning-programs-300640059.html.

"When you visit a school like this, it feels like the future. You get the feeling this is how more of the education system should work." Mark Zuckerberg, quoted in Natasha Singer, "The Silicon Valley Billionaires Remaking America's Schools," *New York Times*, June 6, 2017, https://www.nytimes.com/2017/06/06/technology/tech-billionaires-education-zuckerberg-facebook-hastings.html?_r=0.

In fact, it's more than the annual educational expenditure of any state in the country except New York and California. United States Census Bureau, "2018 Public Elementary-Secondary Education Final Data," last updated April 14, 2020, https://www.census.gov/data/tables/2018/econ/school-finances/secondary-education-finance.html.

Today, a third of millennials believe the Earth may be flat. Hoang Nguyen, "Most Flat Earthers Consider Themselves Very Religious," *YouGov*, April 2, 2018, https://today.yougov.com/topics/philosophy/articles-reports/2018/04/02/most-flat-earthers-consider-themselves-religious.

In 2018, an internal Facebook report revealed that in 64 percent of cases in which a user joined an extremist group... David Gilbert, "Facebook's Algorithm Is 'Actively Promoting' Holocaust Denial Content," *Vice News*, August 17, 2020, https://www.vice.com/en/article/z3e8aw/facebooks-algorithm-is-actively-promoting-holocaust-denial-content.

Until October 2020, when Facebook explicitly banned Holocaust denial, its existence was up to users. Billy Perigo, "Facebook Has Finally Banned Holocaust Denial. Critics Ask What Took Them So Long," *TIME*, October 12, 2020, https://time.com/5899201/facebook-holocaust-denial/.

At any given moment, roughly 570,000 people in the United States are experiencing homelessness. Department of Housing and Urban Development, "2019 Point in Time Estimates of Homelessness," https://www.hud.gov/2019-point-in-time-estimates-of-homelessness-in-US, accessed January 8, 2021.

A 2017 study from the Johns Hopkins School of Health concluded that the more time we spend on social media, the less happy we are. Holly B. Shakya and Nicholas A. Christakis, "Association of Facebook Use With Compromised Well-Being: A Longitudinal Study," *American Journal of Epidemiology* 185, no. 3 (February 2017), 203-211, https://doi.org/10.1093/aje/kww189.

"[We] feel as if [we] are not learning anything"... Kelly Hernandez and Akila Robinson, letter to Mark Zuckerbeg, quoted in Valerie Strauss, "Students Protest Zuckerberg-Backed Digital Learning Program and Ask Him: 'What Gives You This Right?'" *Washington Post*, November 17, 2018, https://www.washingtonpost.com/education/2018/11/17/students-protest-zuckerberg-backed-digital-learning-program-ask-him-what-gives-you-this-right/.

"We're allowing the computers to teach the kids" and "The kids all looked like zombies." Tyson Koenig, quoted in Nellie Bowles, "Silicon Valley Came to Kansas Schools. That Started a Rebellion," *New York Times*, April 21, 2019, https://www.nytimes.com/2019/04/21/technology/silicon-valley-kansas-schools.html.

"I want to just take my Chromebook back and tell them I'm not doing it anymore." Kallee Forslund, quoted in Nellie Bowles, "Silicon Valley Came to Kansas Schools. That Started a Rebellion," *New York Times*, April 21, 2019, https://www.nytimes.com/2019/04/21/technology/silicon-valley-kansas-schools.html.

According to a survey conducted roughly seven months after school lockdowns began... Chegg.org, "COVID-19 and Mental Health," https://www.chegg.org/covid-19-mental-health-2020, accessed January 7, 2021.

"I used to complain every day about having to go to school, but being in quarantine has really made me appreciate being in class." Molly Lawrence, quoted in Henry Dodd, "'I Can't Believe I Am Going to Say This, but I Would Rather Be at School'," *New York Times*, April 14, 2020, https://www.nytimes.com/2020/04/14/us/school-at-home-students-coronavirus.html.

"I'm hoping that things will be back to normal someday." Sasha Udovich, quoted in Henry Dodd, "'I Can't Believe I Am Going to Say This, but I Would Rather Be at School'," *New York Times*, April 14, 2020, https://www.nytimes.com/2020/04/14/us/school-at-home-students-coronavirus.html.

"All these buildings," the governor said, gesturing to the nearly 5,000 schools spread out across his state. "All these physical classrooms. Why, with all the technology [we] have?" Andrew Cuomo, quoted in Naomi Klein, "How Big Tech Plans to Profit from the Pandemic," *Guardian*, May 13, 2020, https://www.theguardian.com/news/2020/may/13/naomi-klein-how-big-tech-plans-to-profit-from-coronavirus-pandemic.

Mathematical Vignette: Health Insurance Markets

Citizen Math Lesson. "Licensed to Ill," *Citizen Math*, https://www.citizenmath.com/lessons/licensed-to-ill, accessed January 11, 2021.

In many countries (including the United States), insurance companies are required to charge everyone the same price for a given policy. Darius Lakdawalla and Anup Malani, "Do You Know What the Affordable Care Act Does? Here's a Primer to Help," *The Conversation*, February 27, 2017, https://theconversation.com/do-you-know-what-the-affordable-care-act-does-heres-a-primer-to-help-73736.

The typical price for an M.R.I. scan in the U.S. is more than $1,400, compared to $450 in Britain. Margot Sanger-Katz, "In the U.S., an Angioplasty Costs $32,000. Elsewhere? Maybe $6,400," *New York Times*, December 27, 2019, https://www.nytimes.com/2019/12/27/upshot/expensive-health-care-world-comparison.html.

Most developed nations provide health coverage to all of their citizens. Max Fisher, "Here's a Map of the Countries That Provide Universal Health Care (America's Still Not on It)," *Atlantic*, June 28, 2012, https://www.theatlantic.com/international/archive/2012/06/heres-a-map-of-the-countries-that-provide-universal-health-care-americas-still-not-on-it/259153/.

Part Six: Inspiring a Society of Reason

Data about coronavirus deaths in the U.S. and Australia. World Health Organization, "WHO Coronavirus Disease (COVID-19) Dashboard," https://covid19.who.int/, accessed January 8, 2021.

...we argue over whether the virus is a hoax... Holly Baxter, "The Americans Who Think that Coronavirus Is a Hoax," *Independent*, May 20, 2020, https://www.independent.co.uk/independentpremium/long-reads/coronavirus-conspiracy-theory-trump-us-hoax-a9498081.html.

At the state capitol in Michigan, protesters surrounded legislators with machine guns... Lois Beckett, "Armed Protesters Demonstrate Against Covid-19 Lockdown at Michigan Capitol," *Guardian*, April 30, 2020, https://www.theguardian.com/us-news/2020/apr/30/michigan-protests-coronavirus-lockdown-armed-capitol.

At the Sesame Place theme park in Pennsylvania, a couple broke an employee's jaw for asking them to wear masks. Janelle Griffith, "Mask Dispute Leads to Couple's Assault on Teen Sesame Place Worker, Police Say," *NBC News*, August 11, 2020, https://www.nbcnews.com/news/us-news/mask-dispute-leads-couple-s-assault-teen-sesame-place-worker-n1236382.

In 2014, the Ebola virus that spread across parts of Africa had a R_0 value of approximately 2... Michaeleen Doucleff, "No, Seriously, How Contagious Is Ebola?" *NPR Shots*, October 2, 2014, https://www.npr.org/sections/health-shots/2014/10/02/352983774/no-seriously-how-contagious-is-ebola.

According to the Centers for Disease Control, the R_0 value for coronavirus is roughly 6. Steven Sanche et al., "High Contagiousness and Rapid Spread of Severe Acute Respiratory Syndrome Coronavirus 2," *Emerging Infectious Diseases* 26, no. 7 (July 2020), https://dx.doi.org/10.3201/eid2607.200282.

...hospitals were full, nurses were overwhelmed, and morgues were renting refrigeration trucks to store the excess corpses. Sarah R. Champagne, "As Texas Morgues Fill Up, Refrigerator Trucks Are on the Way in Several Counties," *Texas Tribune*, July 10, 2020, https://www.texastribune. org/2020/07/10/texas-coronavirus-deaths-morgues-capacity/.

According to a 2020 survey, 61% of conservatives assume that that police officers use the correct amount of force in each situation, compared to just 14% of progressives. 64% of conservatives believe that police officers treat all races and ethnic groups the same, compared to 10% of progressives. Pew Research Center, "Majority of Public Favors Giving Civilians the Power to Sue Police Officers for Misconduct," July 9, 2020, https://www.pewresearch. org/politics/2020/07/09/majority-of-public-favors-giving-civilians-the-power-to-sue-police-officers-for-misconduct/.

Data from Los Angeles Police Department. Independent Commission on the Los Angeles Police Department, *Report of the Independent Commission on the Los Angeles Police Department*, 1991.

According to Chief of Police Medaria Arradondo, leadership knew that Chauvin was an outlier... Curt Devine et al., "Minneapolis Police Are Rarely Disciplined for Complaints, Records Show," *CNN*, last updated June 12, 2020, https://edition.cnn.com/2020/06/11/us/minneapolis-police-discipline-invs/index.html.

Data for Fatal Police Shootings, Total and Fatal Police Shootings per Million graphs. "Fatal Force," *Washington Post*, last updated January 4, 2021, https://www.washingtonpost.com/graphics/investigations/police-shootings-database/.

Between 1980 and 2007, courts in North Carolina convicted 14,500 people of murder and sentenced 328 to death... Michael L. Radelet and Glenn L. Pierce, "Race and Death Sentencing in North Carolina, 1980–2007," *North Carolina Law Review* 89, no. 6 (September 1, 2011), 2119–2160, https://scholarship.law.unc.edu/cgi/viewcontent. cgi?referer=&httpsredir=1&article=4522&context=nclr.

"This is what the best of the old heads meant when they spoke of being politically conscious — as much a series of actions as a state of being, a constant questioning, questioning as ritual, questioning as exploration rather than the search for certainty." Ta-Nehisi Coates, *Between the World and Me* (New York: Spiegel & Grau, 2015).

We've built 100,000 public schools. United States Department of Education, National Center for Education Statistics, 2018, https://nces.ed. gov/programs/digest/d19/tables/dt19_105.50.asp

...500,000 school buses... New York School Bus Contractors Association, https://www.nysbca.com/fastfacts.html

...53 million American schoolchildren... United States Census Bureau, School Enrollment in the United States, 2018, https://www.census.gov/ library/publications/2020/demo/P20-584.html

"The Earth is a very small stage in a vast cosmic arena..." Carl Sagan, *Pale Blue Dot* (New York: Random House, 1994).

ACKNOWLEDGMENTS

Even a personal letter can be a team effort. This letter certainly was. I wish to thank the many friends and educators who generously reviewed "Dear Citizen Math" over the course of its development and offered suggestions for how to make it better. I am especially grateful to Steve Leinwand and Ginny Stuckey, whose encouragement and eagerness to help were unflagging. This letter would not have been possible without them.

ABOUT THE AUTHOR

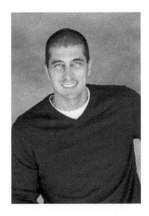

Karim Ani is the founder of Citizen Math, where he develops instructional resources that help students use mathematics to think critically about the world around them. Before that, he was a middle school math teacher and instructional coach. Karim writes and speaks internationally about the role of math education in the 21st century, and was named by *Education Week* as one of the top young leaders transforming education in America. Karim has a bachelor's degree in economics from Stanford University and a master's degree in secondary math education from the University of Virginia. He is a volunteer EMT and avid photographer. When not traveling, Karim can be found under the hood of a late-1970s Toyota Land Cruiser. He tweets from @karimkai.

CPSIA information can be obtained
at www.ICGtesting.com
Printed in the USA
LVHW020817271021
701667LV00004BA/586